# FAN-DOM

## FIC WRITERS, VIDDERS, GAMERS, ARTISTS, AND COSPLAYERS

FRANCESCA DAVIS DIPIAZZA

TFCB

TWENTY-FIRST CENTURY BOOKS / MINNEAPOLIS

TO **LUCINDA AND MARZ**—FOR WALKING TO THE END OF THE
WORLD WITH ME

THANKS TO MY EDITOR, **KELLIE M. HULTGREN**, FOR HER
CLARITY, PRECISION, AND CRAFT

GRATEFUL ACKNOWLEDGMENT TO **JENNIFER MCGEE**, PHD,
PROFESSOR OF COMMUNICATION AT AICHI SHUKUTOKU
UNIVERSITY, JAPAN, FOR SHARING HER WEALTH OF
INFORMATION ON FANDOM HISTORY AND PRACTICES

Text copyright © 2018 by Francesca Davis DiPiazza

Twenty-First Century Books
A division of Lerner Publishing Group, Inc.
241 First Avenue North
Minneapolis, MN 55401 USA

For reading levels and more information, look up this title at www.lernerbooks.com.

Main body text set in Adobe Garamond Pro 11/15.
Typeface provided by Adobe Systems.

**Library of Congress Cataloging-in-Publication Data**

Names: DiPiazza, Francesca, 1961– author.
Title: Fandom : fic writers, vidders, gamers, artists, and cosplayers / by Francesca Davis DiPiazza.
Description: Minneapolis : Twenty-First Century Books, 2017. | Includes bibliographical references
    and index.
Identifiers: LCCN 2017010738 (print) | LCCN 2017027499 (ebook) | ISBN 9781512498875 (eb
    pdf) | ISBN 9781512450491 (lb : alk. paper)
Subjects: LCSH: Subculture. | Fans (Persons) | Mass media—Social aspects. | Mass media and
    culture.
Classification: LCC HM646 (ebook) | LCC HM646 .D57 2017 (print) |
DDC 302.23—dc23
LC record available at https://lccn.loc.gov/2017010738

Manufactured in the United States of America
1-42867-26513-8/7/2017

# CONTENTS

# REPRESENT—
# *HAMILTON:*
# *AN AMERICAN*
# *MUSICAL*

*H*amilton: An American Musical opened onstage in New York City in 2015. A musical about Alexander Hamilton, the US founder who helped create the country's banking system, seems an unlikely hit. But its creator—writer, composer, and performer Lin-Manuel Miranda—composed it in hip-hop rhythms and rhyme. It made history by quickly reaching beyond the usual Broadway theater crowd to attract an international fan base.

Then *Hamilton* fans did what engaged fans of any media do. They wanted more of what they loved, so they made more of it

Lin-Manuel Miranda (*center*) performs with the cast of *Hamilton* at the 2016 Tony Awards. The show won eleven awards that night, including best musical.

themselves and shared it with other people who are passionate about *Hamilton*. Their creations include new and altered stories about the musical's characters, as well as animations, song lyrics, artworks, costumes, and even illustrations for a video game. Love of *Hamilton* and the burst of creative output it inspired illustrate how a modern media sensation becomes part of the wide world of fandom.

## WHAT IS FANDOM?

Fandom is a community of people who share a passion. Originally used to describe the state of being an avid follower of something, the word *fandom* now also describes the collective followers of a particular media source, or "fan domain." Each of these fandoms has its own culture, with rules and expectations. This book uses the word in both senses, focusing on people with a passion for media-based storytelling. Media fans dive deep into books, movies, television shows, video games, and comics, among many other sources, and transform them into new content. In a syllabus for a college course, media scholar and fan Henry Jenkins defined fandom as "the social structures and cultural practices created by the most passionately engaged consumers of mass media properties." Video blogger Dan Howell, in his humorous video "FANDOMS," shared a more personal description with his six million YouTube subscribers: fandom is "one of the most amazing . . . forces on this earth," he said. "You can like something so much that it actually destroys your life." Howell illustrated his point by filming himself slumping to the floor, wondering what to do with his life after finishing the last Harry Potter book.

One of the hallmarks of fandom is that it's easy to join in. Anyone can make fan stories, videos, costumes, visual art, and other creations—known as fanworks. As more and more people have access to the Internet, smartphones that record sound and video, and computer editing tools, it's easier than ever to share and access fanwork online. Fandom has grown into a kind of creative, participatory democracy—or, as fans say, a huge sandbox where everyone can play. As with any community, there are problems: sometimes "everyone can play" is an ideal rather than a reality, and hostilities break out. But the fandom ideal is to empower people to build on their passion and find others who share it.

*Hamilton* itself can be seen as a fanwork. As fan journalist Aja Romano put it, "It's literally a creative text written by a fan that reinterprets or expands upon a previously existing source material." Lin-Manuel Miranda drew on different sources to create an entirely original work. His inspirations included Ron Chernow's biography *Alexander Hamilton* and Hamilton's many writings, as well as the experiences of Miranda's Puerto Rican father in New York City politics. Hamilton's rivalry with Aaron Burr reminded Miranda of the old-school, sometimes deadly rivalries between rappers such as Biggie Smalls and Tupac Shakur in the mid-1990s.

## TYPES OF FANWORKS

Fan-written stories based on existing media, called fanfiction, or fic, can be read in the millions on sites such as the fan-run *Archive of Our Own (AO3)*. In fact, the musical *Hamilton* is similar to a genre of fanfiction called real-person fic. Miranda mostly stuck to historical facts, but fanfic writers are under no such limitations. They take the story further, or deeper, or into an alternate universe. Thomas Jefferson in a pink space suit on Mars? Hamilton and Jefferson in a romantic relationship? Debates about which Hogwarts house each character would join if they attended school with Harry Potter? (No one suggests hotheaded Hamilton is a Hufflepuff.) Variations of all these scenarios exist.

Like *Hamilton* itself, fanworks based on the musical are an every-which-way mashup of media, history, and genres, an intersection of genders, races, and imagination. A teenage fan who goes by the username GinnyWeasley calls herself "a huge musical nerd." She said, "My fandom that most takes on social injustice is *Hamilton*, and they have an entirely PoC [people of color] cast, and it makes you think about how most of our country was built on nonwhites. I think that it really makes you think about history and how we never talk about the PoC who were even more important than the famous white men."

Another type of fanwork is fan-made videos, or fanvids. These are film clips set to music, or fan-produced versions of favorite media, often hosted on YouTube and other video-sharing platforms. For several years, *Hamilton* was available only as live theater—there was no film footage to make into fanvids. That didn't stop intrepid video makers, or vidders. They made their own animated vids or set the songs to clips from other sources. In the vid "If Lin-Manuel Miranda Wrote *High School Musical*," YouTube user huffley6 created a visual pun by pairing footage of high school basketball players with Miranda's song "My Shot," about leaving a mark on history. Some vidders make animated storyboards, edited and set to music. Filmmakers call these storyboards animatics. YouTube user kimi kohi created the vid "the room

# REPRESENT!

Besides presenting different kinds of fanworks, this book will offer a glimpse of the ways fans supply the diversity missing from the media sources they love. When researchers analyzed 414 US films and TV shows for their ratios of gender, race, ethnicity, and sexual status in 2016, their report "Inclusion or Invisibility?" found that invisibility won. Only 18 percent of stories cast girls and women in half of the speaking roles, even though slightly more than half of the US population is female. Only 7 percent of movie casts matched the country's 38 percent nonwhite population (including Hispanic people, a group the US census counts as white). TV was slightly more equitable, with 19 percent of programs proportionately representing the diversity of race and ethnic groups in the United States. The study also found that only 2 percent of speaking characters were identified as lesbian, gay, bisexual, or trans. It did not even touch on the limited representations of religions, body shapes, abilities, social classes, and more.

*Hamilton* made headlines by casting mostly black and Latinx actors and giving women prominent roles—and evoked a powerful response. *Hamilton* fan and self-proclaimed Nerd of Color Kendra James wrote, "Characters that look like me are few and far between. . . . These American heroes have been reimagined to look like the people who actually did (and continue to do) the majority of the heavy lifting that made America what it is." But Miranda did not write any LGBTQ+ characters for his musical, so fans began creating content depicting the characters in same-sex relationships, some of which Miranda has approvingly reblogged. With their creations and their active lobbying of media producers, fans are changing the face of media.

where it happens (animatic)," using Adobe Flash animation software, one of many free apps and programs available to make simple animations. Within nine months, kimi kohi's vid, set to Miranda's song "The Room Where It Happens," had more than one million views.

Costuming is a popular kind of fanwork, with fans creating looks ranging from detailed historical replicas to robot suits, aliens, and gravity-defying outfits, makeup, and hairdos. They meet up at costume balls, game events, and fan conventions, or "cons," such as the huge San Diego Comic-Con. A fan costumer—called a cosplayer—might make an eighteenth-century dress like one worn by Eliza Schuyler in *Hamilton* and then take on that role while walking the floor at a con, acting out how Eliza would react to meeting the Doctor from *Doctor Who* or comic book character Black Widow. Or the characteristic dress might be reenvisioned as a space suit or reinterpreted in the style of an animated show.

In a real-life mashup, fan Kendra James left the New York Comic-Con to line up outside the Broadway theater where *Hamilton* was showing, hoping to win a lottery drawing for a ticket to the sold-out show. While she waited with hundreds of other people, Miranda came out to give the weekly "Ham4Ham" street performance, in which he and various guests entertained the hopeful fans. Still dressed as the character Rey from *Star Wars: The Force Awakens*, James volunteered to perform the fastest rap in the show, "Guns and Ships." Other fans recorded and uploaded this and other Ham4Ham performances, sharing them with the fan community.

Fan artists create a head-spinning array of visual arts, from digital paintings to decorated cupcakes. Many post their work on blogging and art-sharing platforms such as Tumblr, which Miranda fondly said was like the Internet's arts-and-crafts cabin. Fan artist Pati Cmak channeled the vast feelings the musical gave her to draw *Hamilton* in the style of a Disney animated movie. Twitter user danielledejesus1 painted a portrait of actor Leslie Odom Jr. as Aaron Burr on the ten-dollar bill, in place of the usual image of Hamilton. Inspired by a song about Hamilton's children, sna_nabila drew a portrait of them (commenting that she should have been studying for high school final exams instead). Many depictions of the Schuyler sisters show them as the animated trio the Powerpuff Girls. Searching "Fan Art: Hamilton" on art-sharing site DeviantArt returns thousands of results. It's not half a million, like a "Harry Potter" search turns up, but it's impressive for musical theater.

Gaming fandoms can be a world in themselves, with practices ranging from modifying existing games and gaming equipment to designing new ones. Freelance artist Nitya Chirravur, for example, designed graphics for an old-fashioned Nintendo-style *GameforHam*. In one illustration, "Winter Ball of 1780, Level 1," the player has to move Eliza Schuyler across the dance floor to meet her future husband, Alexander Hamilton. As of this writing, game designers have not yet made a full *Hamilton* video game or RPG (role-playing game), but if a fan can dream it, someone will make it.

## FAN ROOTS

Love of *Hamilton* has brought a lot of new faces to fandom, but fandom's history goes back centuries. For example, what we think of as fan writing—changing someone else's tales or creating stories based on them—has been around for thousands of years. But much of contemporary fandom has its roots in science-fiction fandom of the 1930s. People even had a saying for it: Fandom is a way of life. (They shortened it to the acronym FIAWOL, pronounced FEE-a-wall.) These fans felt that reading, watching, and creating works in response to media was more than just a hobby, and they found others who shared their enthusiasm. But for many years, being a fan was deeply uncool. Any high

## *HAMILTON* FANS ON HIS SIDE

*Hamilton* fans have affected US culture in one uniquely public way. Alexander Hamilton's portrait is the face on the ten-dollar bill. Before 2015 the US Treasury Department planned on replacing him with an American woman. But organizers of a "Women on 20s" campaign proposed updating the twenty-dollar bill instead, and Lin-Manuel Miranda got behind the movement. It called for swapping that bill's portrait of Andrew Jackson, a slave-owning president who drove American Indians from their land, with abolitionist Harriet Tubman. The Treasury announced that feedback from *Hamilton* lovers had changed its mind. Tubman will appear on the front of the twenty, with Jackson moved to the rear. On the one-hundredth anniversary of US women's suffrage in 2020, the ten-dollar bill will show women demonstrating for the right to vote on the back. Hamilton will remain on the front.

school student wearing a *Star Trek* T-shirt in the 1970s risked getting slammed into a locker.

Perceptions of fans changed a lot toward the end of the twentieth century. By 2015 a research study on behalf of the broadcasting industry reported that 97 percent of respondents aged eighteen to twenty-four said they were a fan of something. What sparked the change? Google researchers point out that members of Generation C (a cross-generational group, the majority under age forty, that embraces online life) thrive on creation, curation, connection, and community. Community is key to fandom. Social media sites such as Tumblr and Reddit, as well as online forums and fan-run sites, facilitate friendship and the exchange of ideas and do-it-yourself instructions. Topics of identity and social issues, such as gender, race, social class, sexuality, and the transition to adulthood, arise alongside discussions about spaceships and relationships.

# A NOTE ON SOURCES

Fandom is as wide as the Internet. Unlike mainstream media, it provides space for people to express themselves as creators and critics. This book, however, is short. It is a sample platter of fan voices and practices, but there isn't enough room to cover even a fraction of fandom communities. Most examples here come from a few large, long-lasting fandoms, such as Jane Austen, *Star Trek*, *Star Wars*, and Harry Potter, whose fans have produced and continue to produce a wide range of fanworks. Pop culture is fleeting, with today's fan favorites disappearing tomorrow. The sources may change, but fan practices remain much the same. If somebody loves a story, no matter how obscure or outdated, some corner of fandom probably celebrates it.

## "I DIDN'T CHOOSE THE FANDOM LIFE. THE FANDOM LIFE CHOSE ME."

—INTERNET MEME

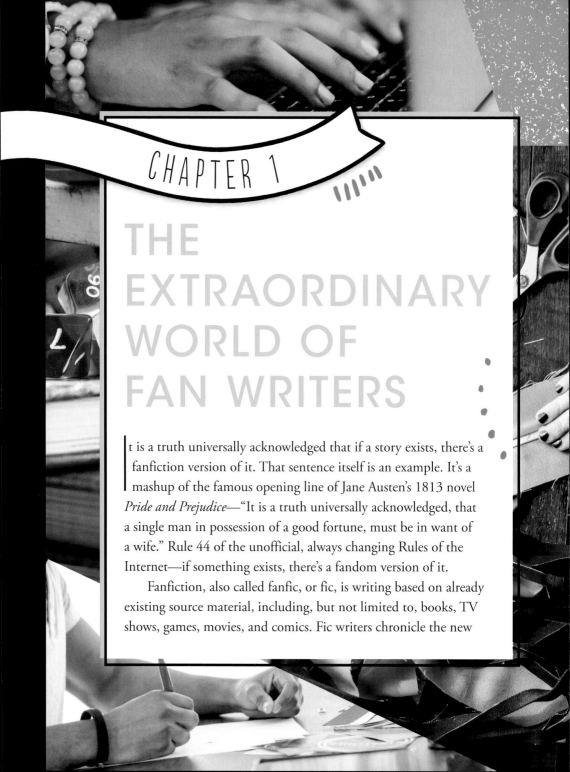

# CHAPTER 1

# THE EXTRAORDINARY WORLD OF FAN WRITERS

I t is a truth universally acknowledged that if a story exists, there's a fanfiction version of it. That sentence itself is an example. It's a mashup of the famous opening line of Jane Austen's 1813 novel *Pride and Prejudice*—"It is a truth universally acknowledged, that a single man in possession of a good fortune, must be in want of a wife." Rule 44 of the unofficial, always changing Rules of the Internet—if something exists, there's a fandom version of it.

Fanfiction, also called fanfic, or fic, is writing based on already existing source material, including, but not limited to, books, TV shows, games, movies, and comics. Fic writers chronicle the new

Anyone can write fanfiction! Some people write just for themselves, while others share and discuss their work in busy online communities.

or altered adventures and relationships of characters and their story worlds. Writers may send characters traveling through time and space, to face dragons or to work in a coffee shop, or imagine them falling in love, maybe in a crossover with characters from another source. Fic might pair Sherlock Holmes with Black Widow (Marvel Comics's Natasha Romanova), for instance, as well as Black Widow with Dr. Joan Watson from *Elementary*, a TV show that changes the Sherlock Holmes character Watson from a white British man to a Chinese American woman. It may bend or swap characters' genders, races, cultures, or other characteristics, such as a male Wonder Woman or a South Asian Rapunzel. Fic also includes nonfiction writing, such as an essay about vampire biology, an exploration of the physics of the sonic screwdriver in *Doctor Who*, or reviews of movies and commentary on games.

The genre is far from new: fanfic belongs to a long

tradition of participatory storytelling. Professor Henry Jenkins says, "If you go back, the key stories we told ourselves were stories that were important to everyone and belonged to everyone." An ancient stew of tropes, or common storytelling devices and themes, inspired and continues to inspire retellings. Among the longstanding stock characters are vampires (Dracula and *Twilight*'s Edward Cullen), tricksters (Robin Hood, DC Comics's Joker, and Harley Quinn), and orphans (Jane Eyre and Harry Potter). Fic writers re-present magicians (Morgan Le Fay and Gandalf the Grey) and logicians (Sherlock Holmes and *Star Trek*'s Mr. Spock). Today, blockbuster media entertainment is the source of most fic. The fantasy role-playing video game *Dragon Age* and the TV show *Supernatural* have dominated fic in the 2010s. But there's room for tiny, rare, and seemingly outdated fandom sources too. Does the Trix Rabbit, who has been denied a bowl of cereal in advertisements since 1959, ever get to taste any? There's fic about that.

The desire of readers and viewers to enter into, expand upon, or change a story from the official version fuels fanwork. Teenage fan Julia Osmon explained, "Fans take a storyline they really like and they tweak and change it to be the way they want it to be." She usually reads fic from the site FanFiction.net on her smartphone, especially stories about characters in the Percy Jackson and the Olympians book series. Fans write fanfiction for love, for other fans, and (due to personal preference as well as copyright restrictions) for free. According to the *New York Times*, "As long as fan fiction writers don't try to sell stories based on copyrighted works, they can write and post them legally."

Fanfiction was once a small, self-published expression of love for a story world. But during the 1990s, the tidal wave of Harry Potter fandom, combined with the rise of the Internet, pushed fic into mainstream culture. Since then fan stories have appeared by the millions on online fic-sharing platforms, fan sites, and forums. They can be as short as one-hundred-word "drabble" or as long as a multivolume series. Fic is considered a literary genre of its own, like science fiction, Western, or romance, though it can draw from and even mash up other genres.

# LITERARY CRED

Anyone can self-publish fic. Its quality varies wildly, and it hasn't enjoyed the highest reputation in literary circles. Fans, however, are quick to point out that fanfiction has a noble pedigree. Sometime before 29 BCE, Roman author Virgil lifted Aeneas, the hero of his epic *Aeneid*, from a much older tale, the *Iliad*, by Greek storyteller Homer. And Homer's epic was composed by many people—we could even call it crowdsourced. Bards had been retelling the tale about the Trojan War for a long time, possibly hundreds of years, before it was credited to Homer around 700 BCE.

Adam Nicolson, author of *Why Homer Matters*, described the process in a way that could apply to fic too. "I think it's a mistake to think of Homer as a person," Nicolson said. "Homer is . . . a tradition. An entire culture coming up with ever more refined and ever more understanding ways of telling stories that are important to it. Homer is essentially shared."

What literary scholars call the intertextual use of Homer—one text borrowing from another—didn't end with Virgil. The characters made their way from the Mediterranean world to what is now Great Britain. There, around 1135 CE, Geoffrey of Monmouth expanded on the *Aeneid*. In Geoffrey's book *The History of the Kings of Britain*, Aeneas's grandson Brutus leaves Rome and travels to an island inhabited only by a few giants. He kills the giants and names the land Britain, after himself. His royal descendants include King Arthur, whose life story Geoffrey tells in racy detail. Geoffrey claimed he was merely translating an ancient text. His fellow historian and contemporary William of Newburgh scoffed, "It is quite clear that everything this man wrote . . . was made up, partly by himself and partly by others either from an inordinate love of lying or for the sake of pleasing the Britons."

Ever since, the Arthurian legend has spread and morphed. A bridge of stories spans from Geoffrey to the medieval *Canterbury Tales* by Chaucer to Marion Zimmer Bradley's feminist retelling *The Mists of Avalon* (1983) to the British TV show *Merlin* (2008–2012) to the 2017 film *King Arthur: Legend of the Sword*. Each has its fic-writing fans, and there is no end in sight.

# JANEITES

British author Jane Austen (1775–1817) began to write as a teenager by mimicking and creating parodies—humorous exaggerations—of the romance novels of her day. (Parodies remain a popular form of fic.) She went on to anonymously publish six novels. Her books were quite popular at the time, but most readers thought them light entertainment rather than serious literature. But Austen, who began her literary career as a fanfic writer of sorts, soon became one of the first published women writers known to have had an actively engaged, interactive fan base.

By the end of the nineteenth century, members of the literary elite calling themselves Janeites declared Austen to be one of the great writers of English literature. British writer Rudyard Kipling, whose hypermasculine characters tromp around the British Empire, was a fan. He read her stories to his family and even visited Bath, the site of an Austen novel, to reread her novels there. He also wrote a story, "The Janeites," about a group of soldiers during World War I (1914–1918) who form a secret Austen fandom. Though one soldier in the story says that Austen's books "weren't adventurous, nor smutty, nor what you'd call even interestin'," another declares, "There's no one to touch Jane when you're in a tight place." According to his biographer, Kipling wanted to capture "the sense of fellowship felt by people who shared a powerful joint experience—whether fighting in war, or membership of a Mason's Lodge, or even familiarity with the works of an author such as Austen." The power of shared experience is a big part of fic.

# SHERLOCK HOLMES AND THE GAME

Sherlock Holmes stories are one of the first sources of fanfic in the modern sense: amateur stories based on copyrighted source material. (Legal protection of original work didn't exist until Great Britain passed

NEW YEAR FICTION NUMBER

THE **STRAND** MAGAZINE

A. Conan Doyle    Arnold Bennett
Denis Mackail   Edgar Jepson   Cosmo Hamilton

A NEW **SHERLOCK HOLMES** STORY

Most of the sixty Sherlock Holmes tales appeared in the *Strand*, which printed fifty-six Holmes short stories and one novel in serial form. Two of the remaining three were novels, and the last appeared in another magazine.

the first copyright law in 1710.) Arthur Conan Doyle wrote sixty adventures featuring his famous detective Holmes, most of them serialized in the *Strand Magazine* between 1891 and 1927.

In 1893, tired of the character, Conan Doyle killed Holmes off. Holmes fans were outraged, and they let the author know it in letters. Then, in a classic case of fans wanting more of what they love, they wrote their own stories, which they called pastiches, a word borrowed from French. Some, in what modern fans call fix-it fic, found ways to resurrect Holmes. Conan Doyle eventually brought Holmes back—but by then an influential fandom had been born.

Sherlockians named or invented many practices that modern fans still use, such as the key concept of canon. They took the word *canon* from the world of religious scholars who pored over the Bible and other ancient texts and hotly debated what was official—that is, canon—and how to make sense of pieces that didn't seem to fit. In fandom, *canon* refers to works by the creator of a source. Fans generally include the creator's public pronouncements as well as their published work. It is canon, for instance, that Voldemort killed Harry Potter's parents. It is also canon that series character Albus Dumbledore is gay. Although author J. K. Rowling didn't state that in the books, she declared it so later. (By bringing Holmes back to life after decisively killing him off, Conan Doyle anticipated the practice of retroactive continuity, or retcon, which is the official replacement of a previously established detail in canon with a new one.)

Holmes fans also created the practice they called the Game: treating the stories as historical documents about a real detective written by his real friend, Dr. John Watson. In the Game, Conan Doyle is just their literary agent. Modern fans know the Game as the "in-universe" point of view, which treats a story as if it were all real. Sherlockians called nonfiction commentary on and discussions about the Sherlock Holmes stories the Writings on the Writings. In modern fandom, this kind of bird's-eye view is called meta, a philosophical term meaning "beyond."

## "WE LIVE IN AN ENTIRELY NEW WORLD": LETTERS AND ZINES

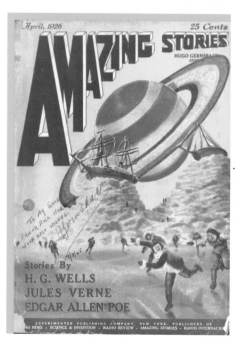

Early Janeite and Sherlockian fandoms were small and rather exclusive. Fandom began to spread more broadly after publisher Hugo Gernsback started *Amazing Stories* in 1926. It was the first US magazine devoted to science fiction—or scientifiction (*scientific + fiction*), as Gernsback called it—and it would further the careers of Isaac Asimov, Ursula K. Le Guin, and many other famous authors.

The first issue of *Amazing Stories* featured cover art by Frank R. Paul. Publisher Hugo Gernsback autographed this copy to a fellow science-fiction fan.

In the first issue, Gernsback appealed directly to fans to get involved: "How good this magazine will be in the future is up to you. Read AMAZING STORIES—get your friends to read it and then write us what you think of it." Crucially, Gernsback added something new to the usual Letters to the Editor column: he printed the addresses of letter writers along with their letters. For the first time, fans could contact one another directly. Inspired, the magazine's fans—most of them male— exchanged letters, met in person, formed clubs, and argued with one another in print. It was much like Internet fandom but in slow motion. By connecting fans, Gernsback planted the seeds of the fan community.

In the 1930s, fans began to make their own magazines. These do-it-yourself publications are called fanzines (from *fan* + *magazine*) or just zines. Most contained some combination of fic, reviews, and essays by fans, as well as letters from readers. Collections of fan letters were called letterzines. In the vibrant science-fiction culture of the time, "fanzines were the social glue that created a community out of a worldwide scattering of readers," according to fan historian Camille Bacon-Smith. Made on the cheap, zines were often mimeographed on 8½" × 11" typing paper, folded and stapled. Mimeographs were hand-cranked duplicating machines that forced smelly purple ink through a hand-typed stencil. Zines passed from hand to hand at local fan clubs or conventions, or they circulated through the mail. Their price covered printing and mailing costs.

In the mid-1950s, the publication of J. R. R. Tolkien's *Lord of the Rings* (LOTR) trilogy sparked another long-lived fandom and helped create modern fantasy as a genre for adults. Excited fans used zines to discuss Tolkien's characters, speculate on the evolution of orcs and forging techniques for magic swords, and write their own stories set in Middle Earth. The first organized Tolkien fan group, called the Fellowship of the Ring, formed in 1960 and published a fanzine, *i-Palantír*, containing articles, original stories, and even a musical.

# THE RISE OF THE MEDIA FAN

Science fiction and its fandom had been male-dominated for decades, but in 1966, the TV show *Star Trek* busted it wide open. Women, kids, college students, and fans of all stripes claimed the show as their own, attracted by plots that went beyond typical sci-fi of the times. Following the voyages of the starship *Enterprise* as it explored the universe in the twenty-third century, *Star Trek* plots were often thinly veiled commentary on hot topics at the time, including US military involvement in Vietnam and the struggle for civil rights at home. The show's hopeful view of the future struck a chord for many.

The crew of the starship was multiracial, and women held positions of power: at the time, these qualities seemed almost as strange as spaceships and aliens. Lifelong *Star Trek* fan Caryn Elaine Johnson, an African American, was nine years old when the show premiered. When she saw Lieutenant Uhura, a black officer, on the spaceship, she recalled, "I went screaming through the house, 'Come here, Mum, everybody, come quick, come quick, there's a black lady on television and she ain't no maid!' I knew right then and there I could be anything I wanted to be." Johnson grew up to be Oscar-winning actress Whoopi Goldberg.

Fans talked about *Star Trek* in person, formed clubs, and wrote to pen pals they found in magazines. They also began to write their own stories based on the show. Thirty years before the Internet, there was no easy and obvious way to share fanfiction. Zines dedicated to *Star Trek* sprang up, to be swapped at cons and mailed to fan clubs.

Women were the pioneers of this new fandom. Editors Devra Langsam and Sherna Comerford printed 350 copies of the first issue of the first all-Trek zine, *Spockanalia*, in 1967. Named for Spock, the half-human science officer from the planet Vulcan, the ninety-page zine published fans' stories, art, lyrics, and commentary exploring the character and his culture well beyond what the show offered. "A Proposed Model for the Vulcan Heart," by Sandra Deckinger, RN, included a medical illustration of this alien organ. In "The Vulcan Gambit," Shirley Meech analyzed the chess games

Spock is seen playing in the show. The zine also published letters from show creator Gene Roddenberry, writer D. C. Fontana, and others involved in the series. Roddenberry gave copies of *Spockanalia* to his staff for insight into viewers' reactions, the way present-day showrunners might look at fan sites.

# SHIPPING

*Star Trek* inspired fan writers to explore the inner workings of the characters. These writers, many of them women and girls, wrote character studies and action/adventure stories, supplying missing scenes and follow-ups, and fixing or parodying elements they didn't like. They wrote about relationships as well as spaceships, filling in characters' backgrounds and development that the show's writers didn't touch. Fans of another show, the 1990s' *X-Files*, would later give a name to the practice of exploring romantic relationships, or "ships," among characters: *shipping*.

The most famous kind of shipping to emerge from *Star Trek* was slash. Named for the punctuation mark in Kirk/Spock (abbreviated K/S), slash fic explores noncanon romantic or sexual relationships between same-sex characters. (No TV characters were identified as LGBTQ+ until the mid-1970s and then in only a few appearances.) Fan writer Charlotte gravitated toward writing stories about Kirk and Spock in love. "It's the perfect recipe for a great love story," she said. "You have two radically different people from millions of miles apart whose lives fit together perfectly. . . . That's a great friendship story. If you add a sexual element to that, it becomes a great love story, and some of us see that sexual element."

Slash fans were cautious about sharing their work in the face of the era's homophobia. Fan Shelley Butler recalled her discovery of slash in an interview years later: "I was going to all the Star Trek conventions in the Los Angeles area," she said. "I began to see . . . fanzines with 'those' covers—artwork showing Kirk and Spock in an intimate embrace or just looking at each other. I was intrigued and started hearing about this very subversive genre called

K slash S. At this time, K/S was barely tolerated even by Star Trek fans, in fact, it was looked down upon, if not hated outright. Everyone in K/S had to be very discreet." They kept writing, however, and the practice of exploring "what if?" relationships spread to other fandoms as well.

Fanzines grew in popularity, and as fans found new stories to share, new fan communities popped up. When the film *Star Wars* came out in 1977, a new group of fans began to produce zines and hold cons. Cheree Cargill founded the *Southern Enclave* (SE) letterzine for *Star Wars* fans in 1983. In the first issue, she wrote, "We hope you enjoy SE and will feel inspired to . . . and send us . . . reviews, zine listings, consumer news, etc. SE is designed to be your sounding board, an instrument for fans to communicate with other fans." It also stated, "No public backstabbing allowed." Fans wrote to discuss (sometimes in great detail) their favorite *Star Wars* movies, and the letterzine remains an active community after going online in 2000.

# MOVING ONLINE

At the dawn of the Internet era, in the early 1990s, fans began to find one another online through Usenet groups, bulletin board systems, e-mail listservs, forums, and chat rooms. The fan community grew, and soon it was as easy to connect with fans on the other side of the world as it was to meet up at the movies. TV and other media fandoms provided a common language, allowing fans to bond and create community.

Jane Austen fic writers were early adopters. The *New York Times* noted that in 2000, Austen's was "the only classic literature to inspire a sizable collection of online fan fiction." Ann Haker, founder of Austen.com, summed up the call of fandom when she explained, "Fanfic writers make no claims to be able to reach the literary heights of Miss Austen, but we feel the need to expand on the world, the characters and the stories, that she created. There just is not enough of Jane Austen's own words to read, so we write our own." Some Janeites insist on fic that is true to Austen's voice and worldview. Others move her stories to different times and places or mash them up with other fandoms, such as the TV show *Buffy the Vampire Slayer*.

Discussing favorite worlds with readers, commenters, and other writers encourages friendships as well as writing. Seventeen-year-old Katie Gowen, who wrote fic about the boy band One Direction (1D), said, "What's amazing is I'll post a chapter and an hour later I'll have, like, eighty comments. I like being able to know that there are people who are reading what I write." She uses the platform Wattpad, a commercially owned site geared toward mobile use.

**"THERE JUST IS NOT ENOUGH OF [JANE AUSTEN'S] WORDS TO READ, SO WE WRITE OUR OWN."**

**—ANN HAKER, FOUNDER OF AUSTEN.COM**

Face-to-face fan networking is thriving too. High-schooler GinnyWeasley only spends about an hour a day online. "I mostly just talk about my fandoms in person with my fellow fangirls at school," she said. She swaps recommendations about her favorites, which include the TV show *Doctor Who* and the musical *Hamilton*. "It's an awesome feeling to come into school," she said, "and just see the wonderstruck look on their face as they explain where they are in the story."

# COPYRIGHT AND MAINSTREAMING FANFIC

US copyright law protects creators' original work from theft. To allow for creative development and freedom of speech, however, the law also permits the "fair use" of copyrighted material. Four factors determine fair use. The new work must transform the original work, it must not use a substantial part of the original, it must not damage the original creator's ability to make money from the work, and because you can't copyright facts, the law grants more leeway in using nonfiction works than fictional ones.

Unless it literally copies the original work, which is plagiarism, fanfic is generally considered "transformative," and therefore legal, fair use of original material. Especially if fic is not published for money, many people in the entertainment industry support fanwork, considering it free advertising for their media.

Individual authors vary on how they feel about fic. J. K. Rowling has said she welcomes it—within limits. A spokesperson for her literary agency said, "Our view on Harry Potter fan fiction is broadly that it should be noncommercial and should also not be distributed through commercial websites. Writers should write under their own name and not as J. K. Rowling. Content should not be inappropriate—also any content not suitable for young readers should be marked as age restricted." Some writers ask that fans not write fic at all.

Anything published before 1923 is no longer protected by copyright and is in the public domain—that is, it is free for anyone to use. Modern works based on copyright-free sources are a booming genre for fanfic and commercial publishing alike. Dozens of professional authors and moviemakers retell and sell Jane Austen's romances, for example. Austen's *Pride and Prejudice* gets a modernized homage in the bubbly Bridget Jones books and movies. The same tale is mashed up with horror in the 2009 book and 2016 film *Pride and Prejudice and Zombies* and is Americanized to good effect in the 2016 novel *Eligible*. Fans consider stories written with the intent to be professionally published to be "pro-fic," not fanfic.

Some fic writers rework their fic to publish it professionally. Cassandra Clare wrote highly popular Harry Potter and Lord of the Rings fanfic, which she deleted before publishing the urban fantasy novel *City of Bones*, first of the Shadowhunters series. It follows the adventures of Clary Fray, who learns on her eighteenth birthday that she is a Shadowhunter, a human with angelic blood destined to secretly protect humans from demons. The series, which reused some of her fanfic, was adapted for film and an ongoing TV series.

The Shadowhunters series was a huge success, as was E. L. James's best-selling, erotic *Fifty Shades of Grey* and its sequels, which started as AU (alternate universe) fanfic based on the Twilight young-adult romances by Stephenie Meyer. Publishers began to scour fanfic sites for new authors. They found Anna Todd, a twenty-three-year-old 1D fan who wrote on Wattpad

Author Anna Todd wrote much of her first fic, *After*, on her smartphone. Since she revised it for publication, it has been translated into more than thirty languages.

as Imaginator1D. In her alternate universe, 1D member Harry Styles is not a sweet-natured singer but a hard-drinking college boy who begins a love-hate relationship with naive Tessa. Soon Todd's fic, *After*, was drawing serious numbers of readers. Between shifts at her waitressing job at Waffle House, Todd wrote and messaged other Wattpad users for hours a day, usually on her phone. "The only way I know how to write is socially and getting immediate feedback on my phone," she said.

When her fic had racked up eight hundred million views, publishers competed for the rights to print it. Todd negotiated a six-figure book and movie deal and worked with an editor to revise and expand the story, including changing Styles's name. (Fans call name changes for copyright reasons "filing off the serial numbers.") Some 1D fans were angry at Todd for going commercial. But, Todd says, "I still feel the most at home in that fandom."

Many fic writers are not looking to become professional writers. They prefer working within fandom culture, valuing the give-and-take with other fans. Fic writer Mithen explains, "Writing fanfic is not necessarily a warm-up for other things. . . . It CAN be, but it involves a totally different set of challenges. You can scrimp on physical descriptions of characters, for example, but using canon deftly to create allusions that will have impact on the readers is a challenge that most writers of original fiction don't run into."

Some writers write fic even after they find professional success. Rainbow Rowell is the author of best-selling young adult (YA) novels, including *Fangirl*, a novel about a teenager, Cath, whose fanfic about Simon Snow, a Harry Potter–like wizard, is hugely popular with fans. When Cath goes to college, she must balance her rewarding online life with her real-life social anxiety and shyness. After *Fangirl* was published, Rowell went through a period of depression and found that writing fic helped. She took a break and wrote a thirty-thousand-word Potter fanfic based on some of her own real-life issues as a parent. "It's Harry and Draco as a couple," Rowell said, "who have been married for many years, and they're raising Harry's kids." She never posted it online, though she has shared parts of it at readings. In writing fic, she regained her joy in writing.

# TYPES OF FANFIC

Fanfic falls into several different types, some of them overlapping. Gen, or general fic, is any fic that does not focus primarily on romantic or sexual relationships. It may be a plot-driven piece involving something as serious as the death of a major character, or it may be just a piece of fluff. Parody and satire, which poke fun at the original material, are popular too.

AUs place characters in different places or times. They come in various flavors. One kind may change just one detail but otherwise stay within the canon. For instance, what if no major characters died in *The Hobbit*? Another AU fic may turn everything on its ear. In the popular coffee shop–type AU, for instance, characters work in or frequent a coffee shop. In a *Hamilton* coffee shop AU, Alexander is a law student and the server at his favorite espresso place is Thomas—Thomas Jefferson. Fic writer Mithen says of these, "It's all about the appeal of translating the unusual into the 'mundane' and finding the magic in it there anew."

Crossover AUs mix different fandoms. "It's great when you can have completely different fandoms and make references and connections between them," says Ginny Weasley. In a Hogwarts and *Star Trek* crossover, for instance, *Star Trek* characters could attend the school

> **"MY PROBLEM ISN'T THAT MY FAVORITE CHARACTERS AREN'T REAL; IT'S THAT I'M NOT FICTIONAL. . . . IT'S NOT THAT I WANT THEM *HERE* WITH ME IN THIS MUNDANE AND ORDINARY WORLD; IT'S THAT I WANT TO JOIN *THEM* IN THEIR EXTRAORDINARY ONE."**
> —INTERNET MEME

for magic with Harry Potter, or Hogwarts students could attend Starfleet Academy.

Brad O'Farrell calls the crossover fic he writes "sort of absurdist. I like writing crossover fanfiction because you can see the story happening, but the two things are so completely unrelated." His favorite fic, "Beverly Drive Chihuahua," is a crossover of the dark movie *Drive*, starring Ryan Gosling, with the family comedy *Beverly Hills Chihuahua*. Both movies are set in Los Angeles and involve heists, but otherwise are opposites. "I just made Ryan Gosling fall in love with a chihuahua," O'Farrell said. "I guess the stupider the crossover is, the more I think it's funny." Crossovers can mix two, three, or more fandoms, and multifandom crossovers can get really wild.

Slash remains one of the most popular fic categories and is still written primarily by fans who identify as female. Almost any media fandom has slash, although the punctuation mark is often replaced with mashed-up character names. Popular pairings on *AO3* come from the TV shows *Supernatural* (Dean/Castiel, mashup name Destiel) and *Sherlock* (John Watson/Sherlock Holmes, or Johnlock). The Captain America movies gave rise to Steve/Bucky, or Stucky. Slashing female characters is less common.

Though LGBTQ+ relationships are still few in mainstream films, more and more canon sources include them. The animated TV show *Legend of Korra* broke new ground in children's television in 2014 when it ended with Korra beginning a romantic relationship with her female friend, Asami Sato. *AO3* hosts about three thousand Korra/Asami Sato fic, including "Jurassic Avatar," a crossover with the Jurassic Park book and film series. Its author, westoneaststreet, describes it as "Legend of Korra . . . with dinosaurs!" *AO3* hosts about another three thousand fic about Nico di Angelo/Will Solace—Solangelo—that are also based on canon in the Percy Jackson books.

Fic about male/female relationships is called het. But as mass media gradually expands its presentation of genders and sexualities, lines between these fic categories blur. Some fans no longer use the terms *slash* or *het*. They simply note whether a relationship is canon or noncanon. A fic writer who goes by Skylar Dorset started writing *Doctor Who* fic because she wanted to see more of the canon relationship between the Doctor and his traveling companion Rose Tyler. Dorset said she felt she "was only being told half the story," so she started writing the other half . . . and didn't stop until she'd written one million words (ten novels' worth) and had brought the couple to "a happy place," with three grown children.

In genderbent, or genderswap, fic, a writer changes a character's sex. Genderbending can help make up for the underrepresentation of girls and women in mass media, especially in roles of power. "It kind of annoys me there's not a lot of strong female leads," Julia Osmon says. A fan of the Percy Jackson and the Olympians series, she makes up for the lack by reading fic that recasts the male characters as female. "I like genderbent fanfic, like fem!Percy," says Osmon. The exclamation point marks a changed trait in fic, such as making Percy female. (A Captain Kirk with wings, for instance, would be winged!Kirk.)

# TROPES AND PROMPTS

Fic writers use many literary tools in their works, including tropes, which are common literary themes or devices. Tropes are used across fandoms and fanworks, and some fandoms even develop their own unique tropes. The podcast (digital audio show) *Fansplaining* is produced by, for, and about fans. In one episode, hosts Flourish Klink and Elizabeth Minkel discussed the results of a survey in which 7,610 respondents voted and commented on 144 fanfic tropes. The survey found that the favorite trope was the classic "friends to lovers," in which friends fall in love. Another familiar trope, the slow burn, teases the reader as characters secretly pine for one another . . . for a long time. Fluff is, as it sounds, light and happy fic. Also in the top ten is the opposite of fluff: the hurt/comfort trope, a kind of intentionally disturbing darkfic in which one character takes care of another who is physically or emotionally wounded. The most hated trope was noncon, short for nonconsensual sex, such as rape or the complicated issue of love potions. Among other most disliked tropes was centaurification, turning a character into a half-human/half-horse centaur. The *Fansplaining* hosts were baffled as to why this trope inspired so much disdain.

To generate stories, fic writers often use and exchange prompts, or fan-generated story ideas. For example, Tumblr user the-fifth-movement shared a fic-writing prompt that invites writers to explore the experience and backstory of Buck Vu, a character from the scary, sci-fi TV series *The OA*, who is a transgender young man in high school. The idea is, "Buck is probably the only trans kid on the swim team at LHS [his school]. Is he allowed on the boys team like he's allowed in boys choir? If so, is he allowed to wear just his binder [a chest-flattening top] and trunks? Or is he forced to be on the girl's team, forced to wear a body suit that makes his dysphoria [feeling of being assigned the wrong gender] 10x worse????" The show also vividly and sometimes disturbingly portrays other real-life issues that spur fan discussions, such as self-harm and trauma survival.

Ian Alexander was a fan long before he landed the role of Buck Vu in *The OA*. He advocates for better representation in films and on TV, giving more fans the chance to see themselves on-screen.

Vu is played by fifteen-year-old Ian Alexander, a Vietnamese American actor who is trans. Alexander shared the swim-team prompt on his Tumblr *lilskeletonprince*, encouraging fans who were excited to see trans characters played by trans actors gaining visibility in canon. In an interview, Alexander said that he is excited by the fans' creative responses. "That used to be me," he said, "someone creating and sharing content about shows they like. Now, I see it happening with something I'm involved in. I want to encourage it as much as I can."

In a few decades, modern fanfic has gone from a handful of stapled, mimeographed pages to billions of digital words. With so much to choose from, fanfic readers value the tradition of creating lists of recommended reading, or recs. In the introduction to the forum for Harry Potter fic, Reddit user NedryOS wrote, "Like all art, it's whatever you make of it. It's humorous, it's a power fantasy, it's emotional, it's sad, it's dark, it's erotic, it's silly, and more often than not, it's really bad. For every Picasso and Rembrandt there's a thousand pseudo-students poorly imitating Bob Ross's happy little trees. But finding the gems among the rubble is worth the effort."

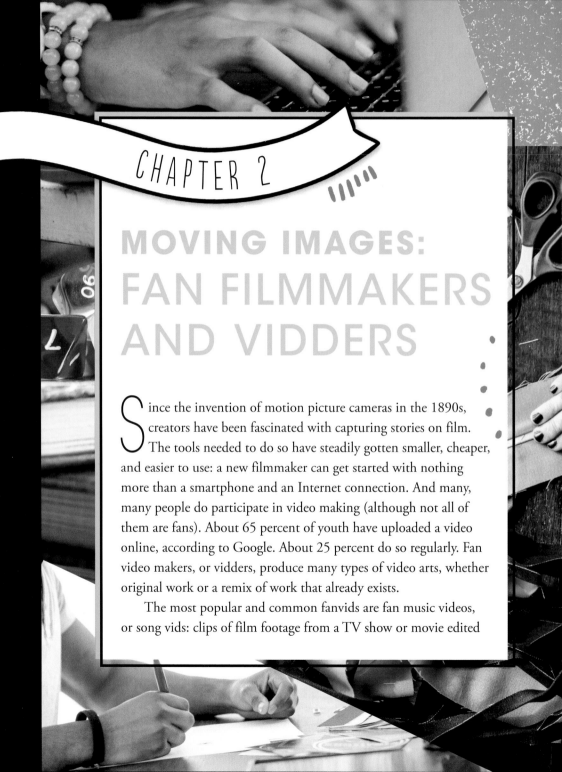

# CHAPTER 2

# MOVING IMAGES: FAN FILMMAKERS AND VIDDERS

Since the invention of motion picture cameras in the 1890s, creators have been fascinated with capturing stories on film. The tools needed to do so have steadily gotten smaller, cheaper, and easier to use: a new filmmaker can get started with nothing more than a smartphone and an Internet connection. And many, many people do participate in video making (although not all of them are fans). About 65 percent of youth have uploaded a video online, according to Google. About 25 percent do so regularly. Fan video makers, or vidders, produce many types of video arts, whether original work or a remix of work that already exists.

The most popular and common fanvids are fan music videos, or song vids: clips of film footage from a TV show or movie edited

Vidders make anime music videos, or AMVs, by fitting clips from a show or shows to the lyrics and music of a song. AMVs might remix sources, mash them up, or just celebrate a favorite fandom.

and set to a song. For example, anime music videos are clips from Japanese animation set to music. Fanvids may also be meta, including reviews and commentary on how mass media handles social issues.

Other fan filmmakers re-create their favorite media. These may be as simple as kids acting out *Star Wars* in their backyard or as complex as fan productions with professional-quality sets, costumes, and actors. As filmmaking tools have become smaller and easier to use, fans have moved in two directions, some making short and quick-to-make vids, such as microvids only seconds in length, and others making longer productions, including full-length films. Fan editors work with the original media to change, restore, or add material.

# EARLY FAN FILMS

Self-taught artist Joseph Cornell (1903–1972) created the first-known fanvid—or, as film historians call it, a repurposed, remixed work of avant-garde cinema. Cornell was a film fan, going to the movies almost daily near his home in Queens, New York, and making sophisticated collages of his favorite actresses from photos in movie magazines. He also collected early films and bought discarded film footage from junk dealers who sold it for its silver content. In 1936 Cornell made his first reedited film, *Rose Hobart*, by cutting up film from the low-budget adventure movie *East of Borneo* (1931) and rearranging its seventy-seven minutes of footage into seventeen minutes featuring its star, Rose Hobart. He first showed his film at an art gallery, projecting it through a blue filter at a slow speed, which gave it a dreamy quality. He accompanied it with up-tempo music from a record called *Holiday in Brazil*. Cornell went on to make about thirty short films of collaged clips from old Hollywood movies and found film footage. His film, paper, and sculptural collages had more effect on the art world than on pop culture, however.

# THE BIRTH OF A FAN ART FORM

Amateur filmmakers invented the idea of tribute movies, in which they remake a film in their own, usually low-budget, way. For about eighty years, until the invention of home video players, the only way to see movies on demand after their theater run was to rent the heavy, fragile film reels from studios. Allan Kohl, who was a teenager in the early 1960s, joined other students in his high school's Cinema Appreciation Club in raising money to rent movies and show them using their school's projector. Then, with money from babysitting and yard work, he and a few friends bought an 8mm film camera to make their own versions of films they liked.

Inspired by movies about radiation-spawned monsters, such as Godzilla, the Japanese King of the Monsters, Kohl set out to make his own live-action movie: *Stinko: The Sewage Eating Monster*. "We made Stinko's head out of papier-mâché over chicken wire," Kohl said, "with Ping-Pong balls for eyes." Filmmaking was expensive and time consuming. "You couldn't see what you were filming," Kohl said. "You sent the film off to the developers and waited ten days to see if it worked."

If it worked, the long strips of film had to be cut apart and the different shots pieced together into one movie. Kohl recalls, "I cut the film with a pair of scissors and then pasted the ends together with film cement. I had to

Filmmaker Allan Kohl made *Stinko: The Sewage Eating Monster* and other films with his 8mm film camera. He went on to become an art librarian and historian.

hold down each splice on the editing block for two or three minutes to let it dry. *Stinko* was approximately forty-five minutes long, more or less. Each showing might take longer because the film often broke at the splices."

## TWISTED BUSTER KEATON

In 1980 aspiring young filmmaker Debbie David created animated short films based on her fascination with Buster Keaton. A silent-film star, Keaton was famous for his stony face and comic yet graceful moves. David made puppets of the actor from paper and twist ties, painted and clothed each one to match Keaton's movies, and filmed them in stop-motion. In this technique, the animator poses each puppet, films a shot, moves the puppet a fraction, films again, and so on. Edited together, the shots create the illusion of movement. Puppet Buster battles billiard balls and sways from a subway car strap. The work is detailed and time consuming. In an interview with *Comedy* magazine, David said, "When something fascinates me, people think I tend to go a bit overboard. Maybe I do, to them, but for me it becomes an intense analysis. . . . The material and the spiritual are united."

Kohl showed the film several times to friends and family. Without any way to distribute it further, he retired it to the basement.

*Star Trek*, with its large, diverse, and networked fan base, was responsible for another burst of fanvid production. In 1975, thirty years before YouTube, *Star Trek* fan Kandy Fong created what many consider the first fan music vid. She did not have the equipment to make a moving-picture film. Video cassette recorders (VCRs) were newly available for home use at the time but were still a costly luxury. She made her fanvid with slides of still images instead.

Fong had met her future husband, John Fong, at a newly formed *Star Trek* fan club in 1974. Among his prized Trek memorabilia were shoeboxes full of clipped and discarded film from *Star Trek*'s editing room. Fong recalled, "We really needed something different to show at a club meeting. There was a popular filk [fan folk] song 'What do you do with a Drunken Vulcan,' and I suggested that we pick out pieces of film that seemed to go with the song. Several of the club members and I used a cassette to record the song. John made the film pieces into slides so we could show it at a club meeting. I would follow the words along in a script and 'click' the single projector at certain words. It was

## FILK: THE MUSIC OF FANDOM

Music has always been a part of fandom, and fans create music to celebrate and even poke fun at their favorite works. At the earliest cons, fans gathered with guitars and hastily copied song sheets to sing lyrics about sci-fi topics set to familiar tunes, called filk. (The word *filk* is thought to have come from a typo in a 1950s article about fans' folk music.) A song sheet from the 1940 Worldcon, for instance, includes "The Road Song of the Transport Cadets," a song inspired by a Robert Heinlein story and set to the tune of "The Roll of the Caissons." A modern example is "Dark Arts," a Harry Potter filk posted on *AO3* by user errandofmercy. It mashes up Katy Perry's song "Dark Horse" and Snape's speech in a Defense Against the Dark Arts class. Filk has expanded from a few funny ditties to a huge collection of rewritten and original music about favorite stories and new worlds. It even includes meta works about being a fan, such as Mo Mo O'Brien's "I'm in a Fandom—Parody Song" on YouTube.

very popular." Fong went on to show this and other fanvids she made at dozens of Trek cons. Her work inspired other fans to make and show their own vids.

# THE VCR ERA

As VCRs became more affordable in the 1980s, vidders taught one another how to edit TV shows and movies into vids. Then they shared their work for free among their friends, at conventions, and even by mail. Like fic, fanvids make transformative, fair use of copyrighted material. Even without the legal restriction on making a profit from copyrighted material, fan culture has always been what anthropologists (people who study human beings) call a gift culture. Participants freely share their knowledge and creations without expecting anything in return.

Vid making with VCRs was laborious. In 1990 three female fans from the vidding group the California Crew filmed the actual process, creating a metavid (a vid that comments on fandom) about meeting in a member's home to make a vid one weekend before a con. First, they browse a pile of videotaped episodes of the TV show *Quantum Leap* (1989–1993). The hero of this time-travel show could appear as people of different ages, genders, and races, making it perfect for fanworks.

Then the crew members carefully choose scenes, noting the location and length of each on paper. One of the vidders has lugged her 40-pound (18 kg) VCR with her and plugged it into her friend's VCR. After they choose all the scenes and calculate the times with a stopwatch, the crew plays each scene on one VCR and records it on the other. Since there's no way to edit the final vid, they must play the clips in the order they will appear. The audio track—the song "Pressure," by Billy Joel—is laid down last, a stopwatch ensuring that the song and video sync up. The vidders take a humorous view, showing themselves falling asleep at the worktable, empty soda cans piled nearby.

The early vidding community was close-knit and made up of mostly women and girls. A fan had to hunt around to figure out how to get involved. Vidders met and kept in touch by mail. They showed their fanvids and shared vid-making techniques at small, fan-run cons. When Internet access became widely available in the 1990s, communication moved to e-mail, forums, and mailing lists. However, there was still no good way to share video online. Vids were still shared at cons, person to person, and in the mail. A British fan who goes by daisiestdaisy recalled how much fans depended on one another, "pre-YouTube, pre-Google, pre-broadband, pre-DVDs even." As a fan of the 1970s US buddy-cop show *Starsky & Hutch*, long popular with slash fans, she said, "I only got to see the show at all because someone I knew from a fandom mailing list copied six of her favorite episodes onto a VHS tape and mailed them to me from the US, which still amazes me with how generous that was."

Not long before the launch of YouTube in 2005, nineteen-year-old Gary Brolsma made the first video that went viral online. He filmed himself dancing in his desk chair, lip-synching to a peppy Romanian pop song. Brolsma posted his video, "Numa Numa Dance," to Newgrounds, a site that mostly hosted Flash animation. "The video was originally intended to make a few friends laugh by just goofing off," he recalled. "I decided to throw it up on Newgrounds just for the heck of it, thinking it would be 'blammed' (automatically deleted for a low scoring video). Little did I know it would wind up featured on their homepage and explode in views."

The *New York Times* marveled at the vid's two million views, unheard of at the time for an online video. (Eventually it reached more than seven hundred million views.) TV news vans turned up outside Brolsma's house. Journalist Diane Sawyer commented on her TV program *Good Morning America*, "Who knows where this will lead?"

The ability to share videos online led to a global wave of innovation and connectivity, much of it hosted on YouTube. One of the earliest viral hits on YouTube was Potter Puppet Pals (PPP), a series of vids featuring simple puppets of Harry Potter characters, manipulated by teenager

Neil Cicierega and friends in an old-fashioned puppet show. Their most popular appearance is in the two-minute video "The Mysterious Ticking Noise" (2007). In it, Professor Snape hears a ticking noise and soon finds himself chanting his name in time to the rhythm. Other characters join in for a catchy name rap. One decade and 173 million views later, the Potter Puppet Pals continue to draw Harry Potter fans. In 2016, after the death of Alan Rickman—the actor who played Snape in the blockbuster film adaptations of the books—more than one hundred commenters on "Ticking Noise" said they'd rewatched it upon hearing the news. Commenter Bella Montoya wrote, "The fact that we all came here [to the vid] makes me not feel so alone."

## AS IT SHOULD BE

Three years after YouTube went live, anthropologist Michael Wesch presented a talk to the Library of Congress about the video-sharing platform. Its participatory culture, he said, led to "new forms of expression and new forms of community and new forms of identity emerging." As an example, he played one of the first multifandom vids, "Us," a mashup of clips from more than thirty media sources, from *Angel* to *X-Men*, by a vidder who goes by lim. A tribute to the fandom community—that is, "us"—it included fan-specific references such as images of piles of books about fandom topics. Lim edited the clips heavily, sometimes adding special effects frame by frame. "'Us' is one of the most poetic statements," Wesch said, about how "we can remix this culture that is being thrown at us. We can take it [make it their own], and throw it back."

In her notes on the making of "Us," lim commented on the criticism that like many vids, hers features mostly male characters. This reflects how few good female roles exist in films and TV, lim pointed out, explaining, "I wanted to say how unhappy I am, in general, with representations of women in media, and how little I identify with most of them." She made vids featuring *Star Trek*'s Captain Kirk, she said, not because she wanted to marry him but because she wanted to play an active role in the universe, as he does.

A thread running through fandom has long been the desire to re-present a source "as it should have been"—whether that's a personal vision of how a story or relationship should have gone or a broader vision of what a story world would look like without social inequalities. Jonathan McIntosh made his humorous 2009 vid "Buffy vs Edward: Twilight Remixed" as a feminist critique of the Twilight series. His six-minute vid builds a new story out of two different vampire series, the TV show *Buffy the Vampire Slayer* and the Twilight movies. Buffy is a human high school student who kills vampires. Edward from the Twilight series is a sulky vampire who attends high school. In canon, Edward treats his girlfriend Bella in a way the author intends to be romantic. But McIntosh replaces Bella's smitten responses with reaction cuts of Buffy's sensible ones, showing Edward's actions as just plain creepy. In one scene, Edward follows someone down a dark street; reaction cut to Buffy on a dark street, saying that being stalked doesn't turn girls on. Later, Edward breaks into Bella's bedroom and watches her sleep; Buffy wakes up and pushes him out the window. Finally, Buffy settles the matter with a stake. The video received millions of views and a nomination for a Webby Award, which honors excellence on the Internet.

Shipping is as popular with vidders as it is with fic writers. It offers another way fans can re-present relationships as they might work without social obstacles. "I make vids from a place of longing," said twenty-four-year-old Milkweedy. Her OTP (one true pairing) is the two male cops from the 1970s' *Starsky & Hutch*, which still has small but loyal fandom. She said, "I feel that the way I see them is the reality, and the show itself is sketches." On June 26, 2015, the US Supreme Court ruled that marriage is a fundamental right, recognizing the constitutionality of same-sex marriage. When she heard the news, Milkweedy said, "I really felt, Oh, great, now Starsky and Hutch can get married! I stayed up all night making a vid."

The vid she posted two days later, "Starsky & Hutch: The Wedding," tells a new story by remixing clips from the show of the two men choosing a ring, trying on tuxedos, greeting family members at the airport, opening presents at what appears to be a wedding shower, and even doing a practice walk down the aisle. Set to the song "When We Get Married" by Larry Graham, the edit makes it appear the men are marrying each other.

Athena, a fan of the gory TV series *The Walking Dead*, created what fans call a shipping manifesto. In her vid, "101 Reasons to Ship Carol + Daryl (The Walking Dead)," she lays out the reasons they ship characters by remixing clips of the two characters and sets them to a song ("Shallows," by Daughter), and then she spells it out in subtitles, from "1. They've both suffered," to "101" the way Daryl hugs Carol "like he'll never let her go." More than three hundred commenters agreed, with many adding more reasons. In the video's comment section, Lilly Wayne jumped ahead to "Reason 112 They stay forever together."

# FILM-IT-YOURSELF

Fans not only remix footage of media sources, they also create their own. Dancer, director, choreographer, and YouTuber Todrick Hall creates innovative musical videos, using pop music medleys to retell familiar tales. "Britney and the Beast" retells the fairy tale "Beauty and the Beast" with Britney Spears lyrics, and "Taylor in Wonderland" sets *Alice in Wonderland* to Taylor Swift tunes. One of his most viewed videos is "Cinderoncé," with black performers dancing the story of Cinderella as told through Beyoncé's music. Ladies in ball gowns dance to a song about wanting a wedding ring, "Single Ladies (Put a Ring on It)," at the ball where Cinderoncé meets Prince Charming. They fall in love dancing to the romantic song "1+1." The video has more than five million views.

As digital use moved from desktop and laptop computers to mobile devices such as smartphones, vid making shifted to forms that are easier

Vidders can film, edit, and share vids on a smartphone, using a variety of apps ranging from freeware to professional tools.

to make and faster to view. Bite-sized videos of ten seconds or less are popular on sites such as Instagram. The 2016 song "Store," by Carly Rae Jepsen, became the soundtrack to a burst of these supershort videos. The song is about ending a relationship by saying you're going to the store. Vidders dubbed the chorus over shots of people strutting down the street to a store, dancing in grocery carts, and so forth. Jepsen herself reposted a mini-fanvid that set her song to a clip from the 1987 romantic comedy film *Mannequin*.

Fast and easy to make, microvideos can react almost instantly to the media of the moment. Fans apply the form to old-school media too. For instance, Colleen Evanson is a longtime fan of *The X-Files*, a sci-fi TV series about two paranormal investigators, Fox Mulder and Dana Scully, that ran from 1993 to 2002 and was revived in 2016. Evanson made 236 micromovies based on the original series and shared each six-second-long

"X-Files Abridged" post on Instagram. She describes a typical installment as "a ridiculously brief recap of every episode as told by Mulder & Scully action figures."

# FAN EDITS

Alongside fans who create song vids, parodies, narratives, and commentaries by editing and remixing film footage, some fans reedit entire films. One example comes from Star Wars fan-edit culture. Twenty years after George Lucas made his first *Star Wars* film in 1977, he reedited and rereleased his first three films as Special Editions. Disappointed fans had harsh words for the director's tinkering, saying it did more harm than good. The original versions of *Star Wars* became hard to find, however. Lucas said that in time these versions would disappear. So a fan who goes by Adywan joined others in laboriously reediting the Special Editions to return them to their original form.

The *Star Wars Revisited* site offers the new edit free of charge to people who already own the official releases. Adywan clearly states the project is not for profit, which would be illegal. "It is not for sale, and no one can ever make money on it," the site's sidebar says. "It is done by a fan, for the fans. We ask that you own a copy of the official DVDs before downloading. . . . All rights and respect to George Lucas, who made this universe for us to play in."

Fanedit.org calls itself the home of the fan edits. It links to fan edits and hosts related information, such as rules and guidelines for respecting the original creators and avoiding copyright infringement. Many fan edits aim to show how the original material could be improved. For example, the site links to *Hunger Games: Mockingjay: The Hanging Tree*, a fan edit of the two films made from the final book of the Hunger Games series. Fan editor Jerick cut 88 minutes from the original films' total running time of 259 minutes to make a single, more streamlined film. Jerick described his edit as an "improved narrative" with a "powerful and exciting new beginning and more emotional thought provoking ending."

# WHERE NO ONE HAS GONE BEFORE

In the tradition of amateur filmmakers of the past, vidders still make their own versions of Hollywood-style films and TV. *Star Trek* alone has spawned dozens of fan-produced films and series since its initial release. Some vids are filmed in garages with sets made of cardboard and duct tape. But with the cost of high-quality video recording and editing tech dropping, others aim to make vids as good as professional productions—and that creates new problems.

In 2014 Alec Peters, a Star Trek fan since childhood, turned to the crowdfunding platform Kickstarter for support to make *Axanar*, a film about an obscure character mentioned in a 1969 episode. More than fourteen thousand fans donated a total of more than $1 million to help make a ninety-minute *Star Trek* movie of professional quality in 2016. To meet copyright restrictions, the film would be free to view.

Then *Star Trek* copyright holders Paramount Pictures and CBS sued Axanar Productions for copyright infringement. Peters was surprised because CBS had ignored noncommercial fan productions for decades. "There's never really been a trial over fan fiction before," said lawyer David Kluft, who has written about *Star Trek* litigation. (Legally, fan-made films and video count as "fan fiction.") But Peters's ability to gain financial backing for the project was a new twist. Kluft said CBS sued because Peters was "too good."

In response, Paramount and CBS set forth Guidelines for Fan Films. The rules limited fan filmmakers to telling stories that were no longer than thirty minutes in total, in segments no longer than fifteen minutes each. Rather than face an expensive court battle, Peters agreed to abide by the guidelines. After the settlement, Paramount and CBS said they "want amateur fan filmmakers to showcase their passion for *Star Trek*," and they will "not object to, or take legal action against, *Star Trek* fan productions that are non-professional and amateur, and meet the . . . guidelines."

Two generations of fans have grown up since *Star Trek* first aired in 1966, each with access to new tools for expressing and sharing their love for that series and many other stories. As advances in technology make it easier to produce and share videos, more and more fans are editing, mixing, and creating new visions. Professional-quality tools can yield stunning expressions of fan enthusiasm but also push the boundaries between amateur and pro creations. Vidders and fan-film makers are not likely to stop exploring the brave new worlds of their imagination anytime soon.

> # "BUT, SEE, I THINK THAT SQUEE [DELIGHT] BEGETS SQUEE. [IN FANDOM THERE] IS, LITERALLY, ROOM FOR EVERYBODY. THERE'S ENOUGH JOY TO GO AROUND . . . AND THERE *ALWAYS* WILL BE."
>
> —LIM, "NOTES: HOW I MADE MY VID"

# CHAPTER 3

# THE PLAY'S THE THING: COSPLAY

Cosplay is the art of dressing as a character. Fans cosplay every kind of character, from Jane Austen and *Hamilton* characters in silk or velvet to intricate anime robots, or mecha, made in part with 3-D printers. Real people, such as Star Wars creator George Lucas, are represented too. It's a global phenomenon and a lively subculture within fandom. At fan conventions, cosplayers inhabit their characters for photo sessions and costume contests or just walk the floor, which is an event in itself.

# LONG AGO . . .

The practice of disguising yourself for fun—not for religious, military, or other reasons—has roots that include masquerade balls. These fancy-dress parties, which started in Venice, Italy, during the sixteenth century, became popular all over Europe in the eighteenth century. Revelers wore elaborate masks, some based on stock characters from comic theater.

By 1869 fashion magazine *Harper's Bazaar* was complaining that costumes at large public balls had taken on a scandalous nature: "Female masqueraders have appeared in scanty French dresses, merely tights and a bodice, or else some dashing male attire." The magazines provided modest costume options for girls and women, such as queens and goddesses. For men, suggestions include Harlequin, a traditional jester in diamond-patterned garb. (This character inspired the DC Comics character Harley Quinn.)

Revelers dance at a fancy dress ball in Paris around 1800. The masked man at far left is dressed as Harlequin, a character from commedia dell'arte, the popular Italian comedic theater form that began in the early sixteenth century.

In the 1887 edition of the book *Fancy Dresses Described; or, What to Wear at Fancy Balls*, Victorian author Ardern Holt dedicated 253 pages to dressing up. Most of the entries merely describe what costumes should look like and not how to make them. The book includes some tips similar to those in modern cosplay tutorials. For example, if you wish to dress up as Joan of Arc, the young French woman executed in 1431 for dressing as a man and leading soldiers against the English army, you will need armor. If you don't happen to have a suit of armor lying around, or steel to make it, Holt recommends "cutting out in strong brown paper the various pieces required, copied from an illustrated history, or from Knight's 'Shakespeare,' pasted over with silvered paper, and strips of linen inside [to] strengthen them, so that tapes may be sewn with which to tie them on."

Arthur Conan Doyle, creator of Sherlock Holmes, barely described his famous detective's clothing. The lasting image of Holmes in a greatcoat and deerstalker cap comes from Sidney Paget's illustrations, featured in *Strand Magazine* starting in 1891. The detective and his world have inspired creative cosplay from the beginning. When Conan Doyle threw a fancy-dress Christmas party in 1898, one woman showed up dressed as the racehorse Silver Blaze, from the Sherlock Holmes story of the same name. Conan Doyle himself dressed as a Viking.

Science-fiction fandom, with its fantastic elements, was a natural fit for cosplay. For the first meeting of the World Science Fiction Convention (Worldcon) in 1939, Myrtle R. Jones Douglas, known by her fan name Morojo, designed and made twenty-fifth-century "futuristicostumes" for herself and her boyfriend, Forrest J Ackerman. Modeled after costumes in the 1936 movie *Things to Come*, Morojo's long skirt converted into a cape, revealing satin shorts underneath. Ackerman wore a green satin cape over a shirt and loose trousers.

# MASQUERADES

Elaborate costume contests, called masquerades, soon became a feature of cons. Ackerman reported on the 1956 Worldcon for the sci-fi magazine

*Fantastic Universe*: "The Masquerade Ball was filmed for televising, and was a sight for bugging eyes. Extraterrestrial glamour girls came in spectrumatic colors. . . . Monsters, mutants, scientists, spacemen, aliens, and assorted 'Things' thronged the ballroom floor as the flashbulbs popped."

Starting with three hundred attendees in 1970, the longest-running comic book convention, San Diego Comic-Con, had grown to twenty-five hundred in 1974, the year of its first masquerade ball. By then *Star Trek* fans were also dressing as the show's characters and putting on their own cons.

Japanese students began dressing up as characters to attend manga and anime cons around the same time. Writer Nobuyuki Takahashi needed a word to describe the new practice for an article. The English-language term *masquerade* sounded "too noble and old fashioned," he said. "Finally, we came up with 'cosplay.' The term was a portmanteau [word blend] of 'costume' and 'play.' It was perfect." The word (in Japanese, コスプレ, *kosupure*) appeared for the first time in print in Takahashi's 1983 article about costumes in the magazine *My Anime*.

Fans check in at the first official Star Trek convention, held January 21–23, 1972, in New York. The hugely popular event included a costume contest, space exhibits from the National Aeronautics and Space Administration (NASA), and appearances by series creator Gene Roddenberry and writer D. C. Fontana.

Cons are not the only site of cosplay. Modern-day Janeites of the Jane Austen Society of North America (JASNA), for instance, meet for weekends of lectures, dance workshops, exhibits, banquets, and period costume balls, for which they dress in historically accurate silk gowns or velvet breeches. The JASNA home page quotes from Austen's novel *Emma*, "It is such a happiness when good people get together—and they always do." In honor of the two hundredth anniversary of Austen's death, the Hampshire Regency Dancers hosted a Grand Jane Austen Ball in July 2017, in Winchester, England, near the village where the author lived.

## "MAKE STUFF AND THINGS"

Some costumes are meticulous reproductions of the original. Video game characters inspire some of the most detailed cosplays, complete with realistic weapons. This is a specialty of experienced costumer Bellexi, who described herself on Instagram as "just a girl that makes stuff and things!" To transform herself into Roadhog, a male character from the video game *Overwatch*, she spent seventy hours creating his signature weapon on a 3-D printer. She painstakingly copied the tattoo that covers Roadhog's big, bare belly onto a flesh-colored bodysuit. Wearing the suit under a halter top, she appeared to have a real tattoo on her stomach. With a mask covering much of her face and camouflage pants to complete the look, she won the Best of Weekend for Hall Costumes at the 2016 Anime USA con.

Hall costumes are often worn all day, so most are practical designs for activities such as walking around, standing up for hours, breathing, and going to the bathroom. By contrast, masquerade costumes are worn only in a costume contest, where they are judged on high standards of craft. Masquerade contestants make their own costumes and document how they were made. Designed to be worn for a short time, the costumes are more impressive than comfortable.

While some cosplayers aim to re-create a costume in exact detail, others reinterpret or combine characters. Spider-Man shows up in Captain America's colors, and Elsa from Disney's film *Frozen* appears as Daenerys Targaryen from the book and TV series *Game of Thrones*. Darth Vader from *Star Wars* walks the floor in a vast variety of styles. Instead of his all-black armor, this villainous character might be dressed like a Disney princess, with a pink helmet and mask. There's Darth Vader as perky Pikachu, a bright yellow species of Pokémon, with red cheeks and bunny ears. Steampunk Vader wears a World War I gas

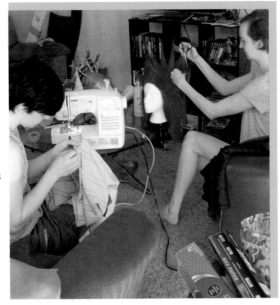

Cosplayers Ash (*left*) and Katie (*right*) re-create costumes from the anime *My Hero Academia*. Anime cosplayers often use wigs and carefully structured clothing to replicate the wild styles of animated characters.

mask and helmet, his chest piece constructed from curly bits of a brass musical instrument. Body painters re-create Vader's suit entirely in paint on bare skin. One young cosplayer in the trademark black mask pilots a wheelchair transformed into Vader's TIE fighter (a single-pilot space vehicle).

Cosplay even extends to noncharacter elements of media favorites. Fans of the BBC show *Sherlock* make costumes out of fabric that looks like Sherlock Holmes's living room wallpaper—a dark brown lily pattern. They may even add Sherlock's famous house address, 221B. Fans particularly love the TARDIS, a spacecraft and time machine from *Doctor Who*. It turns up as everything from a blue-painted cardboard box to a ruffly pinafore dress to a cloth costume on a llama. Costumed pets come to cons too, if only outside the venues. With their flat faces and wrinkly brows, for instance, dogs such as pugs and shih tzus make convincing Ewoks, the teddy-bearlike creatures from *Star Wars*.

Groups of cosplayers may coordinate their costumes. Friends go together as the four Teenage Mutant Ninja Turtles, for instance, or Pac-Man and the enemy ghosts from the old-school arcade game. Whole families might portray existing fictional families such as the Incredibles, a superhero family from the animated movie of the same name. Or they might make up their own family, cosplaying the children of video game characters Mario and Princess Peach as cute mushrooms, like the friendly helpers in the Nintendo games.

Strangers meet and pose with others doing characters from the same series in series-specific photoshoots. Some group cosplay is spontaneous. Fan and costumer Keelin said, "One of the funniest things I've seen at a con

Cosplayers at the 2016 Big Apple Comic Con in New York City gather for a superhero group photo.

was a deliberate cosplay crossover at OSFest in Omaha, Nebraska. All of the 'Doctor' characters—a couple of Doctor Whos, Doc Ock, Doc Brown, Dr. Strange, Dr. Horrible—met up in the lobby and staged an argument over their credentials."

# DREAM IT, BE IT

Cosplayers often make some or all of their costumes. They may spend thousands of dollars, or they may repurpose free or low-cost materials. Others adapt or commission costumes. Cosplayer Roland's Forge is a professional prop maker who has been creating costumes and accessories since 2008. His detailed costume of the villainous Jafar from Disney's *Aladdin* was a fan favorite at the 2016 Anime Los Angeles con. On the other end of the spectrum, a teenage boy cosplaying Alucard, a vampire from the Japanese manga *Hellsing*, decided to make Alucard's long red cape even though he had no idea how. "My aunt gave me her old red dress, and I stayed up all night cutting and sewing it into this coat," he said. "I'd never done any sewing before, so I made lots of mistakes. Don't look at the seams inside."

Crafty types may have an advantage, but as long as a costume stays together during the con, no one needs to know it's held together with hot glue, duct tape, and staples. Beginners don't have to rely on trial and error, however. Online fan-made tutorials give step-by-step instructions on how to achieve effects in costumes and accessories. Want a costume to look as if it survived decades after an apocalypse? Tutorials explain how to distress, stain, and otherwise age fabric. Hair that stands high up in curls? There's a tutorial on building a wire frame to fit your head. Tutorials in makeup arts appeal to fans interested in movie and glamour makeup skills, from wild eyeshadow to film-quality prosthetics.

Inventive fans on a tight budget start with used clothes from thrift stores or friends' closets, whether as costume pieces or for fabric.

Old-fashioned papier-mâché—newspaper strips dipped in a mixture of flour and water and applied to a mold of chicken wire or an inflated balloon—makes a good helmet or mask. Anyone with the patience and hand strength to cut up cardboard cereal boxes can make armor. Foam, such as floor or yoga mats, is lightweight and easy to cut. Styrofoam is stiff enough to carve into props.

Cosplayers usually avoid working with metal, which is expensive and heavy. Most cons prohibit metal props for safety reasons. They also prohibit or limit real weapons, including sharp blades, as well as flames and other fire hazards. Anything that could cause falls, such as skates and slippery glitter, is often forbidden, as are many oversized props, including wings. Before attending a convention, be sure to check its cosplay guidelines. Cosplayers work around these limitations with metallic spray paint, adhesive papers, foam, and creative determination.

Although 3-D printing creates amazingly realistic props, it is complicated and can be expensive. The most common 3-D printers follow software instructions to lay down very thin layers of melted plastic that fuse together. The printers cost from a couple hundred to a few thousand dollars, so some fans use shared printers at libraries or community centers.

The first step is to design or download a model. Sites such as Thingiverse offer patterns and tutorials for 3-D printable objects, from spaceship models to body armor for your cat. Many designers share their work for free. Voluntary contributions help them continue to share amazing work. Fans can also hire commercial 3-D printer services. After the printing comes assembly, gluing parts together, and sometimes sanding—lots of sanding—for a smooth finish. Painting or other finishing is the final step.

Cosplay can be overwhelming, so experienced cosplayers advise newcomers to start small and keep it simple at first. Makeup, wig styling, custom tailoring, and other skills take a lot of time to learn. But anyone can get started with a bit of planning and a trip to the thrift store.

## COSPLAYERS OF COLOR

"Who should I cosplay?" Experienced cosplayers advise picking a favorite character. Looking like the character is not a requirement. There are no rules about race, gender, body type, ability, age, or anything else.

Cosplayer Chaka Cumberbatch believes that "at the very heart of cosplay is the love for a character, and the desire to bring that character to life. That's what it should be about." In 2010 Cumberbatch, a black woman, began cosplaying one of her favorites, Sailor Venus. The character is from the anime series *Sailor Moon*, about a team of magical schoolgirls who guard the solar system. Unable to sew, Cumberbatch worked closely with another cosplayer to design Venus's sailor top, big neck bow, and short flouncy skirt. She carefully chose her accessories, including a wig in the right shade of blond.

At the con, a professional photographer snapped her photo. Thinking nothing of it, she later posted the picture on Facebook. Her photo made the rounds on social media sites, and the racist responses shocked Cumberbatch. She wrote an influential article about her experience on the online magazine *xoJane* titled "I'm a Black Female Cosplayer and Some People Hate It."

"My Venus became the unintentional face of the cosplay race debate online," she wrote. On the one hand was condescending approval, such as, "For a black cosplayer (not to be racist) she did an amazing job!"— suggesting black cosplayers do not normally perform as well as white ones. On the other hand was blatant disapproval, Cumberbatch recalled, such as comments saying "I had a 'face like a gorilla' and wasn't suited for such a cute character, because I am black."

Insults can be enough to scare anyone away from cosplay, Cumberbatch acknowledged, but she urged newcomers to take on the challenge. She went online to create #28DaysofBlackCosplay, a social media event in which black cosplayers post their photos with the hashtag every day during February, which is Black History Month. The conversation continues year-round on blogs such as *Cosplaying While*

*Black* and *The Nerds of Color (NOC)*, where fans can talk about race, gender, class, and other factors in cosplay and fan culture. Reporter Shawn Taylor wrote for *NOC* about the first meeting of the Silicon Valley Comic Con in 2016. He was part of a panel about diversified fandom, noting the rise of many active fan artists of color. Impressed by the many great female cosplayers at the con, Taylor ended his review with a note: "Fellas. You have to step up your cosplay. Women and women-identified cosplayers are running the game."

## COSPLAY AND MODESTY

Another branch of cosplay resists the idea that you have to be willing to show a lot of skin to do cosplay right. This trend has roots in book covers, comics, anime, and other media in which all women wear revealing clothing—some of it physically impossible!—that reflects outdated ideals of sexiness in male-dominated fandom. Realistic armor, comfortable clothes, and cosplay that allows modesty are a growing subset of fan culture—and also turn up in canon sources. For instance, Ms. Marvel, the alter ego of American Muslim teenager Kamala Khan, wears a much less revealing costume than most Marvel superheroes.

Ange, a Muslim cosplayer from Indonesia, incorporated her headscarf into a costume from the Japanese TV series *Kamen Rider Gaim* for a 2017 hijab (headscarf) cosplay event near Kuala Lumpur, Malaysia.

## A PERFECT STORM

Dax ExclamationPoint is a geek and a drag queen whose signature cosplay includes Uhura from *Star Trek*, Hello Kitty, and Marvel Comics's Ororo Munroe—code-named Storm. In Storm's skintight silver bodysuit and a long white wig, Dax was a standout at the 2016 New York Comic Con (NYCC), which boasts some of the best cosplay in the country.

Dax ExclamationPoint was a competitor in 2016 in *RuPaul's Drag Race*, a reality TV show that celebrates the art of drag. Like cosplay, drag is a skill- and performance-based art form. Drag queens are men, frequently gay men, who dress like women for entertainment. They use the pronoun "she" when they're in character.

Dax grew up as a fan of comics and sci-fi and superhero movies, and her geekdom came before drag. "I've always been a huge nerd," she said, "and essentially started drag to be more like Storm or Catwoman." She wants to be known as "the queen of all nerds . . . and tour conventions and hang out with people that love all the campy [exaggerated], geeky, dumb stuff I grew up with that I love, too."

Cosplayers aren't limited to characters who dress or look like them in canon. For example, some cosplayers who wear hijab (headscarf) incorporate it into their costumes. A photo of Dania, username HijabiHooligan, giving a salute as Captain America in an American flag hijab got a lot of love on social media. (Bill Rosemann, creative director at Marvel, the company that owns the character, saluted her back on Twitter.) Makeup artist Saraswati (username QueenOfLuna) shaped and draped hijabs of different colors into the elaborate hairdos and headdresses of different Disney characters. With blue contact lenses, face-paint freckles, and a gold-colored hijab held in place with the character's signature headband, Saraswati became Alice in Wonderland. With her black hijab twined into a turban and an elegant moustache and beard painted on her face, she became Jafar, the bad guy from *Aladdin*. Her photos were a hit.

In an interview with the site *Black Nerd Problems*, Dania said, "There is a lot of stigma surrounding the hijab. I want to show people that choosing to cover up does not deprive me of anything that my fellow women have—I can still have fun without compromising my faith!" In the vast and diverse cosplaying community, she can feel comfortable doing what she loves.

# ROCK YOUR LOOK

Robert Franzese looks almost exactly like Peter Griffin, the overweight, white dad from the adult, animated TV show *Family Guy*. Getting the costume together was easy, Franzese said. He already had a pair of green pants and a white button-down shirt. Acting like Griffin came easily too, and Franzese became a hit at cons around the United States. Seth MacFarlane, creator of *Family Guy*, even retweeted a YouTube video "Real Life Peter Griffin Goes to NYCC 2014." In it Franzese explained one of the appeals of cosplaying. "I have a nobody job, making nobody pay," he said, "but I go to New York Comic Con and people are pulling out phones like I'm freakin' Brad Pitt."

Fan culture generally seeks to be inclusive, welcoming fans of all genders, political and sexual orientations, races, and abilities. A male cosplayer recalled a good reception at New York Comic Con while cosplaying Elsa from Disney's *Frozen*: "I do something called crossplay or gender-bending," he explained. "You've got to take a female character or a male character and then switch it, and then people are like, 'It's very weird.' . . . Luckily it is a very accepting community."

But prejudice exists in fandom too, and cosplayers encounter lookism, or judgment based on physical appearance and abilities. To address this, Franzese appeared on a panel, Body Confidence and Positivity in Cosplay, at NYCC in 2016. The four panelists discussed how cosplayers of every shape and size can stay positive. Franzese said he had a hard time growing up as an overweight kid. The key to positivity, he advised, is to surround yourself with people who lift you up and help you become the best version of yourself. It's the fan reactions and the friendships that make cosplaying joyful. The panel participants urged everyone who wants to cosplay to risk the possible public discomfort and dare to do it.

Valerie Hardt agrees. She began cosplaying when she was a child and has cosplayed a range of types, from Rose Tyler, a heroic love interest from *Doctor Who*, to Raleigh Becket, one of the buff brothers from the movie *Pacific Rim*. Cosplay has helped her to accept her body, she said, adding, "I felt more at home in my own skin after cosplaying as [DC Comics's] Black Canary and Ms. Marvel."

**"COSPLAY ALLOWS US TO BE OUR HEROES. WHICH IN TURN MAKES US REALIZE THAT HEROES ARE JUST LIKE EVERYONE ELSE. ONCE WE REALIZE THAT, THEN WE CAN GO BE HEROES FOR SOMEONE ELSE."**
—VALERIE HARDT, COSPLAYER

Steven and Millie, a retired couple who call themselves the Cosplay Parents, don't let entertainment's focus on young characters restrict their fun. They mostly cosplay older characters, such as General Leia Organa and Han Solo from *Star Wars: The Force Awakens*, and they also make up happy endings for characters who didn't get them in canon. They cosplay Captain America and Peggy Carter as if they had been able to grow old together, and Carl and Ellie from the animated movie *Up*, imagining the couple adventuring together in old age. They never buy entire costumes, preferring to scour thrift stores and raid their closets for materials to modify. Steven said, "The fun and accomplishment is making it yourself." Though they are shy people, they said the positive reception they received at cons encouraged them to keep going. They added, "We were also amazed that people who saw us at the convention or other events, and through social media, have embraced us in that the older generation can cosplay too, and have made comments like '#relationshipgoals.'" The Cosplay Parents advise others not to let negative comments about body type, age, or ethnicity deter them from cosplaying.

## "BE COOL AND BE KIND"

More than ever, girls and women are upping the ante at cons with their enthusiasm for cosplay. Some onlookers, however, react to costumes with rude or sexually inappropriate behavior ranging from name calling to taking photos or touching cosplayers without permission. Derogatory comments are aimed at boys and men too, as well as at anyone dressed as characters of a different race, body type, or gender. To raise awareness and to guarantee cons are as safe and friendly as possible, in 2010 three women began an organization called Geeks for CONsent. It and other groups adopted the slogan Cosplay ≠ CONsent, or Cosplay Is Not Consent.

Since then many cons have adopted antiharassment policies and train their on-site security to respond respectfully. Signs on the show floor at NYCC, for example, remind con-goers to treat one another with respect, reading, "Remember: Cosplay is not consent. Keep your hands to yourself. If you would like to take a picture with or of another NYCC Fan, always ask first and respect that person's right to say no. When at NYCC, be respectful, be nice, be cool and be kind to each other."

## LIVE LONG AND PROSPER

Many cosplayers bring elements of their fandoms into the rest of their lives. *Star Trek* fans Greg and Michelle got married—in costume— during the Star Trek Las Vegas 50th Anniversary Convention in 2016. The groom wore Captain Picard's dress uniform from the show *Star*

Cosplayers at the MCM London Comic Con in 2016 mash up Star Wars and anime with a wedding theme.

*Trek: The Next Generation* (1987–1994). Guests dressed as human and alien characters from the different series. At the reception, figures of characters Riker and Troi topped the wedding cake. Greg showed off his ring, engraved with the starship *Enterprise*. And Michelle's seven-year-old son offered a fan toast: "May my mom and dad live long and . . ." He stumbled on the word *prosper*, but the attendees responded with cheers.

Cosplay, like *Star Trek*, seems set to live long and prosper. And fans' demands for more seem to be inspiring not just more stories but a more realistic variety of humans portrayed in them. Production of *Star Trek: Discovery*, the seventh TV series in the franchise, began in 2017. It features new Starfleet uniforms and another diverse crew: African American actor Sonequa Martin-Green plays the lead, and Chinese Malaysian actor Michelle Yeoh plays a Federation captain. Producer and longtime Trek fan Bryan Fuller says he knows cosplayers will rise to the occasion.

# CHAPTER 4

# PICTURE THAT! VISUAL ARTS AND COMICS

F an art begins where original media sources end. Much like fanfiction writers, fan artists imagine and portray things that aren't in the original work. Fan art includes portraits and tributes, as well as new or re-visioned content. Internet personality Brad O'Farrell describes it as "when you have characters that are from a story or a movie and you want them to be doing things that they don't do, like wish fulfillment, but for the characters." This chapter will be a quick tour through just a few of the millions of fandom-inspired visual expressions, which leap from Hello Kitty cupcakes to 3-D sculptures of video game heroes.

The word *art* can sound intimidating, as if you need a special

Digital drawing pads are used to create and alter images. A single digital pen, or stylus, can mimic not only pencils, markers, and brushes but also photo retouching and video editing equipment.

talent to make it, but fan art relies on the desire to create, not technical ability. Still, many fan artists learn skills that allow them to better convey their own visions.

Fans still use traditional art materials—pencils work great! But intuitive and affordable digital technology opened up art to fans who couldn't afford or didn't know how to make it a couple of decades ago. Bryan Konietzko, cocreator of the animated TV show *Avatar: The Last Airbender* and its sequel, *The Legend of Korra*, commented on the change in fan art over the years. He recalled that "back in the *Avatar* days [2005–2008] . . . the typical fan art we would get [around 2008] would be a charming, childish crayon drawing stuffed in an envelope. Nowadays on *Korra*, I take a skewed screenshot with my phone, post it, and shortly thereafter someone un-skews it, crops it, separates the character levels, clones the background, 'Ken Burns' it [zooms in and pans across the image] with a multilevel slide, animates the characters blinking and talking, tints it, and makes a GIF out of it, that I then see on the same phone with which I took the original picture. Times they are a-changin'."

# IN THE BEGINNING

Fan art has a history as long as fanfiction's. According to art critic Jonathan Jones, "The story of art is largely a story of homages, remakes, rivalrous borrowings, nuanced imitations." Just as Virgil riffed on Homer's tales, artists in ancient Rome made their own versions of earlier Greek art. Throughout the Middle Ages in Europe (500–1500 CE), artists created new images to tell familiar stories, drawing on certain conventions to stay true to the original. In fact, they even used patterns and motif collections to ensure that they included the right people and symbols for each story—like a visual canon.

The medieval (of the Middle Ages) cathedral was like a comic book of the Bible and other sacred stories, created by anonymous artists. Then very few people knew how to read, so churchgoers looked to the cathedral's pictures in stained glass, stone carvings, and more for their story cycles. According to scholar Umberto Eco, the art of the cathedral was "a sort of permanent and unchangeable TV program that was supposed to tell people everything indispensable for their everyday life, as well as for their eternal salvation."

Medieval artists were not bound to the visual canon. Many painted scenes from the Bible as though they took place in their own time, putting figures from the book in fashionable clothing and local settings. Wealthy patrons could even order paintings that inserted themselves into the scenes, alongside saints and prophets of old.

Art history shows that artists around the world have valued the practice of replicating art. Artists in medieval China, for example, learned by copying great artists of the past. The goal wasn't to duplicate the originals but to learn from them to develop one's own style. The famous twelfth-century painting *Spring Festival along the River*, by Zhang Zeduan, is a silk scroll, 10 inches tall by 208 inches long (25 cm by 529 cm). It shows people going about their lives. It has inspired numerous copies over the centuries—including a huge, interactive, digital version in 2010—many of them updated to make the scene more relatable.

# WHERE'S ARTHUR?

The legend of King Arthur has inspired artists as well as writers for centuries. Around 1316, anonymous French artists painted seventy-two richly colored miniatures on gold backgrounds for a book about King Arthur, *La Queste del Saint Graal* (The Search for the Holy Grail). One of the illustrations, "Arthur on the Wheel of Fortune," depicts a common trope: the goddess of luck spins a wheel that governs the fate of individuals. Four figures of Arthur cling to a large wheel spun by a lady in a red dress. On the top, he wears a crown. On the bottom, he is almost naked.

Victorian artists loved Arthur too. The young creators of the Pre-Raphaelite movement, for example, produced many images of the legend—both canon and noncanon. The nineteenth century also brought a new technology, photography. Artists soon turned its focus on fan favorites. In 1874 English photographer Julia Margaret Cameron agreed to create photographs to illustrate Alfred Tennyson's twelve-poem cycle *Idylls of the King*, a retelling of the legend of King Arthur. She recruited family and friends to play the characters, costuming her husband, Charles, as the wizard Merlin. Agnes Mangles played the sorceress Vivien, seducing Merlin to gain power over his secrets.

The sorceress Vivien (played by Agnes Mangles) casts a spell on the wizard Merlin (played by Charles Hay Cameron) in Julia Margaret Cameron's photo illustration for Tennyson's *Idylls of the King*.

Photography at the time was a chore. Sitters had to hold a pose for several minutes while a glass negative coated with light-sensitive chemicals was exposed inside the camera. According to Mangles, Charles kept laughing, ruining many exposures. Cameron developed the glass negatives in her darkroom and made prints by placing photo paper on the glass and exposing it to sunlight. She manipulated her negatives for effect, scratching them or using multiple negatives to print a single picture. Out of 245 exposures, she chose 25 for Tennyson's book.

Arthurian legend remains one of the most enduring subjects of fan art. A recent search for "King Arthur" on the website DeviantArt, an online community for artists and art lovers, returned 20,442 results for all artistic media. Gojirafan made a photo collage of still images from *Monty Python and the Holy Grail* (1975), a very silly movie that pits Arthur against dangers such as the Killer Rabbit. Freakyfir shared a design for video game characters based on *King Arthur and the Knights of Justice*, a cartoon series about a high school football team that goes back in time to fight alongside Arthur. And Tathariel uploaded a realistic pencil and charcoal drawing of Arthur and Merlin as portrayed in the BBC TV show *Merlin*.

## SCRAPBOOKS AND SPACESHIPS

In the early twentieth century, a host of technological changes impacted fan artists. Cheaper full-color printing (and thus the Sunday color comics in newspapers) and affordable mass-market photo magazines, among other developments, gave fans new material and new tools.

One of the first magazines for movie fans, *Photoplay*, debuted in 1912 and quickly grew in popularity, offering pages of pictures of stars on and off the set. Early media fans cut and pasted, hand colored, and collaged photos of movie stars from magazines, newspapers, and other paper media into scrapbooks. "Scrapbooking was the blogging of that period," says Ellen Gruber Garvey, a professor of English at New Jersey City University.

"It has all these parallels to what we do today." For example, modern fans assemble fandom collages in apps and share them on image-sharing sites such as Pinterest.

In general, girls and women have been the most frequent scrapbookers. Lifestyle blogger Maegan Tintari wrote about uncovering her grandmother's scrapbooks from 1934. "She must have been around seventeen years old when she spent countless hours snipping and gluing and captioning the pages of these books," Tintari said. "She added her own color to the black-and-white images." Tintari notes that when she was eleven, she filled similar scrapbooks with clippings of actor Johnny Depp.

In the 1930s, the sci-fi fandom started by *Amazing Stories* magazine got a big cultural boost. Aldous Huxley's best-selling novel *Brave New World* (1932) envisioned a dystopian future where people happily accept totalitarian (dictator) rule. One of the era's many Hollywood monster flicks, *King Kong* (1933), became a megahit. And the space opera comic strip *Flash Gordon* began in 1934—the year many consider the beginning of the Golden Age of Sci-Fi. In this tumultuous era, mass-market publications needed lots of cover art, and artists supplied it. Their colorful and often lurid images of stellar travelers (in skimpy costumes totally unsuited to space travel), robots, bug-eyed monsters, flaming ray guns, rocket ships, and other technological wonders fired the imagination of young fans. Many of them went on to become fan or professional artists—as well as innovators in technology.

The Golden Age of Sci-Fi lasted roughly until the 1950s, the decade when J. R. R. Tolkien published his Lord of the Rings trilogy. Tolkien brought his own work to life with illustrations of dwarves and dragons, hand-drawn maps, and hand-lettering of the script of elves. Besides drawing his own visionary worlds, Tolkien had been something of a fan artist since childhood, illustrating the works of other writers to share with family and friends. He took inspiration from medieval manuscript artists and the intricate designs of William Morris, a prime mover of the nineteenth-century Arts and Crafts movement. Tolkien's art inspired fan artists, who contributed to the huge fandom that mushroomed around Tolkien's work in the 1960s.

As interest in making and sharing fan art grew, con staff took notice. Conventions soon began including art shows, often with categories for amateur, professional, and even child artists. Con-goers could peruse a display of art, including tributes, comics, re-visionings, and original works on fan topics, as well as book covers, animation cels, and props from professionals. Sometimes the art was available for purchase, either direct from the artist or through an auction held at the end of the event. Fans loved the opportunity to see artworks by other fans and to bring home favorites.

## COMICS: "EVERYBODY DRAWS"

For fans of comic book and sci-fi art, the next leap forward came in 1970, when 145 fans met in the basement of a hotel in San Diego, California. It was the first meeting of what would become the nation's leading comics convention, the San Diego Comic-Con (SDCC). From the beginning, the focus was on comic book art and artists. At comic cons, art shows were featured, showcasing all kinds of work, from professional to amateur. At an early con, cartoonist Tom Gill, who drew *The Lone Ranger*, gave a chalkboard tutorial on how to draw comics. This began a tradition of how-tos offered for fans by pro artists. Interactions with these professionals, as well as with other enthusiastic fans, nurtured many fan artists.

The history of comics goes back more than a century and is worth a book in itself. They come in a huge variety of forms, from single-panel gags to print comic books to graphic novels to webcomics running for a few weeks or even years. As a subculture of fandom, comics can be both source material and a type of fanwork. Comics also blur the line between fanfic and fan art, since writers often work alongside artists. But in the end, comics rely on visual storytelling. Comics with no words exist, but not the other way around.

Cartoonist Rebecca Sugar grew up drawing pictures. She said in an interview, "When you're a kid . . . everybody draws, everyone wants to draw, drawing is fun! Everyone who is working in cartoons now drew a lot when they were kids." She continued, "At some point, when you're growing up, someone tells you 'this is not something you can actually do for a living' or 'this is not actually a good drawing.'" But, "As long as you don't stop, you can make as much art as you want."

Sugar did not stop. She kept drawing and then working in comics. In 2013, when she was twenty-five, the Cartoon Network greenlit her series *Steven Universe*. It's about a family of three intergalactic Crystal Gems who protect Earth and take care of a young boy, Steven, whose mother was a Gem. The Gems have no gender (they're magic stones from outer space), but they all present as female and use female pronouns. Some are in romantic partnerships with other Gems. The cartoon became the network's first female-created show and inspires a whole new generation of fan artists. In a winning combination, the characters are fairly easy to draw and the story world is childlike, yet complex.

Self-taught cartoonist Adrian drew a wordless comic, "Lion: Origins." Imagining the origins of characters is a popular creative fan pursuit. In twenty-two color panels, Adrian depicts her headcanon (a fan's personal version) of the unexplained connection in *Steven Universe* between the magical pink Lion and Steven's mother, Rose Quartz. In Adrian's comic, Rose finds a wounded baby lion lying near its dead mother. Rose heals the cub with her tears, which also turn him pink. She visits him as he grows up, and before she says a final farewell, she places some cherished objects in his magic mane.

# BEND IT LIKE HERMIONE

Representation is an important issue in comics and fan arts, as it is in the larger culture. Dwayne McDuffie (1962–2011) grew up as a comic-loving, self-described "proto-nerd" and a "motor-mouthed black fanboy." There were almost no comic book heroes during his childhood who looked like him, McDuffie recalled for the *New York Times*. "You only had two types of [black] characters available for children," he said. "You had the stupid angry brute and the he's-smart-but-he's-black characters. And they were all colored either this Hershey-bar shade of brown, a sickly looking gray, or purple."

After finishing college and graduate school and attending film school, McDuffie landed the job of his fanboy dreams: he became an editor and later a writer at Marvel Comics. His first high-profile project was the Marvel comic sitcom, *Damage Control*, created with artist Ernie Colón, about a cleanup crew that repairs the damage superheroes leave in their wake. Determined to bring well-depicted, diverse characters to comics, McDuffie joined several other African American artists to found Milestone Media, the most successful minority-owned comic company. There McDuffie cocreated *Blood Syndicate*, a comic book about a multicultural crime-fighting crew.

But not all fans have the chance to become creators. Racebending is one creative way fans seek to repair the damage done by racism in existing media. The term was coined as a protest when the 2010 film *Avatar: The Last Airbender* cast a white actor for the main character, who is an Asian boy in the anime-inspired TV show of the same name. Despite fan protests, studios also cast white actors in Asian roles in the 2016 Marvel film *Doctor Strange* and in the 2017 US film adaptation of the 1990s manga and anime *Ghost in the Shell*.

Frustrated fans have renamed the practice of replacing a canon character of color with a white actor *whitewashing*. They use the term *racebent* to mean the opposite: reimagining white characters as nonwhite ones. The website *Racebending* calls for depictions of characters that represent communities of color in "meaningful inclusion in the American storytelling landscape." To do it well, a fanwork should do more than just change the character's appearance: it must realistically reflect how a change in race changes the character's entire social setting.

Occasionally, racebending in fandom leads to change in a story's canon. In her Harry Potter series, author J. K. Rowling described Hermione as a clever girl with frizzy hair and brown eyes. From early on, many fan artists depicted Hermione as a girl of color in illustrations, photosets, and other fan art. Hermione attends wizarding school with Harry, where she faces prejudice as a mudblood—a wizard from a Muggle (nonmagical) family— which fans of color said they could relate to. Tenacious fans even created a popular hashtag, #blackHermione.

Five years after release of *Harry Potter and the Deathly Hallows—Part 2* (2011), in which white actor Emma Watson played Hermione, black British actor Noma Dumezweni portrayed the character onstage in the play *Harry Potter and the Cursed Child*. Rowling gave the casting her enthusiastic support, saying in a tweet that she had never specified Hermione's race. Popular fan artist Marianne Khalil celebrated the new casting, saying, "What's most amazing to me is the palpable influence of the fandom in this. I don't think this could have happened if they hadn't been so vocal."

## SPREADABLE

Photoshop and other editing software programs or apps are a huge part of remix culture, empowering fans to change media to say what they want. Digital manipulation and reproduction of images became possible in 1990 when the powerful and—compared to traditional photography—affordable editing software Photoshop came on the market. This software radically changed visual arts by making advanced techniques easier for amateur artists. Since then many inexpensive digital-art tools have been released. Even the free photo-editing apps on smartphones offer far more options than Julia Margaret Cameron could have dreamed of in her darkroom.

Fan-made digital visuals aren't all exactly what one would call art. For instance, image macros, or block text overlaid on images, are more like potato chips: lightweight, fast, and easy to make on meme-generator sites. Memes spread quickly and often disappear just as fast, but some are quite sticky. An image of the Lord of the Rings character Boromir saying, "One does not simply walk into Mordor," from the 2001 movie *The Fellowship of the Ring*, spawned a zillion image macros bearing some variation of "One does not simply *x*." The meme spread far beyond the LOTR fandom and still pops up more than a decade later—an incredibly long life for a meme. In crossovers (which are as big in fan art as in other fanworks), fans make Doctor Who versions (he does walk into Mordor and gets lost), *Frozen* versions (Elsa does not simply let it go), and more.

# DIGITAL PAINTING AND DRAWING

Digital painting is like traditional painting except the artist pushes around pixels instead of paint. Graphics tablets allow artists to draw directly on the screen with a stylus, which works like a pen, pencil, or brush. The surface registers every tiny shift in pressure, angle, and direction of the writing tool. Sophisticated software blends colors, and brushstrokes lay down layers of texture, light, and shadows.

Ashlee Casey (username AVCasey) is a self-taught fan artist in her twenties. "Sometimes people try to tack on negative connotations when they call someone a 'fan artist,'" she said in an interview. "I don't think it makes you any less of an artist. Art is what inspires, what makes you feel . . . and fan art is definitely of both those things." Casey was working at her cashier job in a small Texas town when the editor of *Iron & Air* motorcycle magazine messaged her about her digital portrait of popular *Walking Dead* character Daryl Dixon posed with a silhouette of a wolf's skull on the red wall behind him. When the editor messaged that he wanted her art for the cover, Casey said, "I stared at my phone for probably twenty to thirty minutes before I could muster up the brainpower to say yes."

Binkk7 is a professional artist who continues her childhood habit of making fan art for fun. "I make fan art for the same reasons probably most fans do," she said, "out of the desire to participate in things I love and to pay homage to characters." Like many fans, she makes more than one kind of art. A fan of *Doctor Who*, she animated Daleks knitting and chanting "extermi-knit" instead of their trademark "exterminate." In a mix of old and new, she photoshopped her dog into *Star Trek* screen captures and made slide-show vids out of them. (In fandom no style is ever defunct if even one fan keeps it alive.)

Borrowing from art history still works too. In a series of black-and-white digital drawings, Binkk7 inserted the zombie-killing Michonne from *The Walking Dead* into medieval Dance of Death scenes. An hourglass sits nearby, reminding the viewer that life is uncertain. The art trope of skeletal personifications of Death dancing with victims was popular in fifteenth-century Europe, when plague was decimating the population. It appealed to Binkk7 because, she said, "the medieval mood was apocalyptic, which is big in our times too. Also, Michonne has this really cool Japanese sword, like the medieval knights who are trying to fight off death with a sword."

Fan artist Binkk7 drew Michonne, from the TV series *The Walking Dead*, in the style of fifteenth-century Dance of Death woodcuts.

Some working artists incorporate fannish references in their professional pieces too. Chicago-based fine artist Debra Yepa-Pappan, for instance, playfully remixed *Star Trek* imagery in her photo-manipulation *Spock Was a Half-Breed (Live Long and Prosper)*. In this colorful piece, the starship *Enterprise* appears in the sky above two teepees bearing the science logo worn by the half-human, half-Vulcan Spock. In the foreground is a nineteenth-century photograph by Edward Curtis manipulated to show an American Indian woman with Spock-like pointed ears giving the Vulcan salute. Like Spock, Yepa-Pappan is mixed race. On her father's side she is Jemez Pueblo, and on her mother's, Korean. She said, "It always amazes me how ahead of their times science fiction shows, movies, novels, etc., were and are, in their use of different technologies and their inclusiveness between different races of people, humanoids, and species." She has shown her manipulated photographs in art galleries. *Spock Was a Half-Breed* was reproduced on the side of a building as part of the Painted Desert Project, hosted by Chip Thomas, a.k.a. Jetsonorama.

## TIMELESS TOOLS

Pencils, ink, scissors, and glue remain popular materials for fan artists. Graphic designer Laurent Beuten challenged himself to blend aspects of every character in the video game *Overwatch* with those of a similar

Pokémon. He drew the mashups with Prismacolor pencils instead of his usual digital tools, explaining on a subreddit that a friend had showed him how the pencils' look lent power to his art. In one illustration, a smiling yellow Pikachu appears to bounce toward the viewer wearing Tracer's goggles, leather jacket blinker belt, and pulse pistol.

Artist Melissa Moffat continues the tradition of cut-and-paste with actual scissors and glue. She makes paper collages, taking days to cut up enough fashion magazines, comic books, and other printed material to make one collage. She organizes the scraps by color, pattern, and shape and assembles them into something like a modern-art puzzle. Her dense and intense images don't tell a story. They reflect the feel of the character. "I like to deconstruct [analyze] the images of the characters and break them down into parts and create a new abstract image," she said. "Like with my *Joker* piece, I tried to channel insanity," she said, "and with [my] Superman collage it was the strength, heroism, and justice." She also made a collage series for *Star Wars: The Force Awakens* using *Star Wars* comic books and glossy tribute magazines.

Mycks Sato, who lives in New Jersey, paints in ink using traditional Japanese brush techniques. Her fan art often incorporates samurai, or Japanese warriors. She uses the name Mycks (pronounced "mix") when she collaborates with her mom, who is a Japanese calligrapher [handwriting artist], and sometimes with her little sister too. Mycks paints their pieces in watercolor and sumi, a type of black Japanese ink. She said, "The inspiration of each piece might come from old Japanese samurai and ninja [stealthy fighters], or more modern pop culture icons such as characters from Star Wars and Lord of the Rings. I am mostly inspired by the brushwork, using traditional Chinese calligraphy brushes, brush pens, watercolor brushes, etc." Her portrait of Tolkien's character Legolas shows him as a samurai archer alongside the Japanese word for *light*, rendered in her mother's calligraphy. A Han Solo–inspired samurai appears with the word for *adventure*, and *Star Wars* hero Rey, wearing a kimono, carries her staff next to the word for *hero*.

Every year InkTober challenges artists to draw with ink throughout October. Jake Parker started the event in 2009 to encourage himself to improve his inking skills. Thousands of artists at all levels all over the world have joined in. The rules are simple: draw something in ink (or pencil and then ink), and post it on social media tagged with #inktober. Participating artists draw whatever they want. Parker supplies a prompt for each day to give artists ideas. Eric Kwun posted *Star Wars*–inspired art twenty-five out of the thirty-one days of InkTober 2016. He recommended the event, saying, "Artists of all skill levels can participate together with no fear of judgment or criticism and just celebrate the art of putting ink on paper and creating some beautiful."

Some fan artists mix traditional and digital arts. Artistiq draws her favorite celebrities with graphite and color pencil on paper. She uploads some of these delicate and realistic portraits into an animation program. When she's done, autumn leaves cascade through the sunlight of pop singer Taylor Swift's hair. An animated hummingbird flits through a cloud of cherry blossoms around Jennifer Lawrence.

# FAN CRAFTERS, MAKERS, AND BODY ARTISTS

Fan crafters are endlessly, mind-bogglingly inventive. They model Dalek chess pieces from clay and paint their refrigerators to look like the TARDIS from *Doctor Who*. They sew Marvel plushies out of felt and crochet pastel squid that look like My Little Ponies. To them, kitchen drawers or bathroom cupboards are repositories of possible crafting materials. A circular lip balm container becomes the *Star Wars* Death Star; a gold-foil-wrapped chocolate makes an excellent snitch from the Harry Potter game of Quidditch. Glass beads + nail polish = *Steven Universe* gems. Little fannish figurines take up residence inside empty jars, living in fan-made habitats there. Comic book pages are pressed into service as covers for shoes, phone cases, and picture frames.

To see just a few samples of the many items created out of one fandom, check out the dozens of ways to make the iconic starship *Enterprise*, from *Star Trek*, on the DIY website Instructables. It appears as a bicycle, a bookshelf, a cake, a climbing tree for cats, and more. User iGreeny constructed the ship from hardware fasteners: wing nuts, bolts, and screws, with a horizontal washer for the ship's saucer. User bchafy employs office supplies: a CD for the saucer, pens with colored caps for the engines, and binder clips. Other projects use gingerbread, yarn, Legos, biodegradable clay made of cornstarch, 3-D printed plastic, and origami paper.

Bodies can be a place to display fan art too. The most elaborate body arts are seen in cosplay, but some fans show their commitment daily with a tattoo. Tattoos may be elaborate and obvious, such as the face of a character on a forearm. Or they may be recognizable only to other fans, such as a small, subtle tattoo of the number 9 3/4, the railway platform where Harry Potter catches the train to Hogwarts.

Fans display less permanent body art in intricate miniatures on their fingernails. JeeA Lee paints intricate designs on her fingernails freehand,

Japanese nail artist Yoko Matsuda used pop culture sensation Hello Kitty as inspiration for her fingertip art.

with a very fine, modified paintbrush. She posts photos of her weekly nail art on Tumblr and Instagram. In one crossover, she painted reindeer antlers on Chewbacca, a hairy warrior from *Star Wars*, on one of her nails. The other nine nails featured Disney Christmas scenes. Fans who feel less confident in their ability to paint ambidextrously can buy decals of images from major fandoms, such as DC or Marvel Comics, to apply to their nails.

# A VIDEO GAME EMPEROR AND A REBEL PRINCESS

Fans also use images from their fandoms to express opinions about real-world issues. It's a way to use media to talk back and say something about yourself. During the US presidential campaign of 2016, supporters of winning candidate Donald Trump made triumphant fan art. A popular meme photoshopped Trump into the *Warhammer 40,000* video game, in which a god-emperor in gold armor protects humanity from cosmic threats. He also appears photoshopped into paintings of Napoleon, George Washington, and even Jesus.

After President Trump was inaugurated in 2017, critics of the new administration also used pop culture to express themselves. Graphic designer Hayley Gilmore captured the mood of media fans who were not fans of the president with a protest poster featuring Leia Organa, a rebel leader from *Star Wars*. Gilmore placed the text "A Woman's Place Is in the Resistance" over a 1977 photo of Leia holding a blaster pistol. After the inauguration, millions of people around the world joined grassroots women's marches to demonstrate in support of human rights. Many of their handmade signs utilized pop-culture quotes and images, from Beyoncé's lyric urging ladies to get in formation to the warning "Winter is coming" from *Game of Thrones*. Printouts of Gilmore's poster, alongside handmade signs featuring Leia, popped up at marches from Los Angeles to London.

Community is often an important part of fan art, and art for the surreal podcast *Welcome to Night Vale Fan* demonstrates a kind of mind meld that can take place within it. The audio-only show claims to be a community radio news broadcast from the desert town of Night Vale, with announcer Cecil reporting on distinctly odd happenings in a deadpan manner. The podcast is supported entirely by fans through donations and sales of T-shirts and other merchandise. With almost no canon descriptions of the characters beyond cryptic visuals such as "a dark hooded figure with unknowable powers," the show is something of a prompt generator. A fanon, or fan canon, has evolved about the main characters' appearances. A lot of fans see Cecil, for example, as a nerdy-looking white guy, wearing a button-down shirt and sweater vest—with a third eye in the center of his forehead.

> **"YOU DON'T HAVE TO WAIT FOR PERMISSION TO MAKE YOUR ART."**
> **—FELICIA DAY, AUTHOR OF** *YOU'RE NEVER WEIRD ON THE INTERNET (ALMOST)*

Fan artist Toril Orlesky, who started posting comics online at the age of twelve, created a series of stark *Night Vale* comics. One image accompanies Cecil's typical *Night Vale* proclamation that no one has seen anything unusual "because all of us are normal!" While it's slightly ominous in the show, that proclamation could be a happy motto for fandom, where artists of all kinds are free to pursue their visions, no matter how strange they may seem to others.

The love of a fandom can keep artists going. Professional artist and longtime SDCC participant Allison Sohn holds popular How to Draw panels at conventions. "I do a step by step," Sohn said of her art-marker tutorial, "taking a drawing of a portrait of a popular film or television character all the way through to final finished colors. I talk about tricks that help, and things to look out for." Asked for advice for beginning artists, she replied, "DON'T GIVE UP!!!!"

# CHAPTER 5

## GO MAKE A GAME!
## GAMES AND GAMERS

Gaming is somewhat different from other fandoms. There's no way even a casual gamer can be an entirely passive consumer, unlike a TV viewer. Playing the simplest game requires the player to do *something*. To some extent, every gamer is an engaged fan. But some gamers choose to enter more fully into active game fandom. This chapter will focus on video and role-playing games, but fans of board, card, and other games participate as well.

Who plays games? Specific numbers on role-playing games are hard to pin down. A 2011 study reported that 91 percent of people aged two to seventeen play video games. A 2015 study found that 49 percent of American adults report playing video games with some regularity. Though both men and women assume that

Finalists face off in the *Street Fighter V* tournament at the 2016 Evolution Championship Series event in Las Vegas, Nevada. More than fourteen thousand fans competed in tournaments for nine different player-versus-player games.

more men are gamers, the same number of men and women play video games. However, men are twice as likely to call themselves gamers.

Pop-culture writer Jonathan Malcolm Lampley commented on the widespread appeal of gaming, "Even the stereotypical high school 'jock' of the 21st century is computer literate and likely plays video games; for that matter, the Internet has given rise to 'fantasy football' and other hypothetical sports games that strike me as far weirder pastimes than collecting action figures or learning the [*Star Trek*] Klingon language could ever be." But gaming's popularity is nothing new.

Game fans, of course, make all the fanworks discussed in earlier chapters. They write fic. In 2015, on *AO3*, fic based on the game *Dragon Age* came in second only to fic from the *Supernatural* megafandom. Game fans make vids, cosplay, and art. Engaged gamers film and upload gaming vlogs (video blogs), game commentary, and reviews. Chat rooms and forums host game discussions. Fans also make their own models and game pieces for tabletop games. They create new games from the ground up, and they modify existing games and game characters.

Games—particularly video games—are a kind of pop art, according to game writer and critic Tom Bissell. In a 2013 interview, Bissell said, "The generation coming of age right now is taking it for granted that the things they watch and read have some type of input/output aspect to them." And the line between fan and commercial producers is fuzzier in games than in other fan activities. Indie—independent or alternative—designers, for instance, make games that may get commercial release or may be shared directly, for free.

Games may be highly mathematical or pure fantasy. In first-person shooter games, the player sees the gameplay from behind a gun. Gamers play fitness games, such as *Wii Fit*, and life-simulation games, such as the Sims series. Puzzle games include *Tetris* and *Candy Crush*. Massively multiplayer online role-playing games (MMORPGs), such as *World of Warcraft*, are the electronic offspring of tabletop role-playing games (RPGs) and live-action role-playing (LARP). LARPers meet in person, too; in a mix of fanfiction, cosplay, and gaming, role-players become their characters, or avatars.

## FROM PAWNS TO PIXELS

Humans have been designing games since ancient times. Four-sided ankle bones from animals served as dice in amusements, games, and divination for thousands of years. The modern children's game of jacks, also called knucklebones, is a descendant.

A complete history of gaming would be far too long for this book. But we can follow one game, chess, from its start in sixth-century India all the way to the beginning of modern video games, and beyond. Merchants carried chess sets from country to country during the Middle Ages, and it became known as a refined pastime that improved players' knowledge of military strategy. Powerful rulers commissioned luxurious chess sets made of precious materials, played long-distance games via correspondence, and even had the game included in their portraits. As the centuries passed, fans produced books and magazines to discuss chess, as well as boards and pieces ranging from tiny and portable to nearly life-sized.

This game board and pieces, possibly for an early ancestor of chess, were found at Mohenjo-daro, an archaeological site in what is now Pakistan. This ancient city, one of the largest in the Indus Valley Civilization, was built around 2500 BCE.

With its simple rules and infinitely complex strategies, chess was one of the first games to be translated into computer language. And the first computer game designers were mathematicians. In 1936 British mathematician Alan Turing came up with an idea for a Turing machine, a computer that could follow any algorithm, or set of rules. In 1948 he created a chess-playing algorithm called Turochamp for such a machine to follow. However, the machine didn't actually exist, so Turing played the role of the computer by doing the calculations by hand. It took him thirty minutes to calculate each of the computer's moves. A computer scientist in the United States played for the humans. The computer lost. In 1957 IBM researcher Alex Bernstein created the first computer chess program that could play an entire game by itself. The IBM 704 computer, which filled an entire room, took eight minutes per move.

Inspired by these early efforts, computer scientists developed versions of tic-tac-toe, tennis, and other games for computers as well. In 1962 a group of student and staff computer scientists at the Massachusetts Institute of Technology (MIT) wrote a hack, or unauthorized program, called *Spacewar!* This space combat game was developed on the new PDP-1 mainframe computer, one of the first to have a cathode-ray tube display, like a TV screen. Steve Russell, one of the creators of *Spacewar!*, later told *Rolling Stone* magazine how he and four friends decided to design a flashier way to show off the computer's features. "Here was this display that could do all sorts of good things!" Russell said. "We decided that probably you could make a two-dimensional maneuvering sort of thing, and decided that naturally the obvious thing to do was spaceships." Within weeks *Spacewar!* spread to other PDP-1 computers at research centers around the country. The program encouraged users to refine it, and students and staff alike eagerly added new features. The 1972 *Rolling Stone* article described *Spacewar!* as "a flawless crystal ball of things to come in computer science and computer use."

The same article quoted a definition of these new computer programmers, called hackers, from Xerox researcher Alan Kay. "A true hacker is not a group person," said Kay. "He's a person who loves to stay up all night, he and the machine in a love-hate relationship. . . . [Hackers] tended to be brilliant but not very interested in conventional goals. And computing is just a fabulous place for that." The term *hacker* did not have connotations of illegal activities at the time. Rather, it referred to people so passionate about computer programming that they did it for fun, possibly using institutional computers without permission.

## ARCADES AND LIVING ROOMS

For moving images, bright colors, and sound effects, gamers went to video arcades to play games on machines throughout the 1980s. The gameplay didn't allow for much narrative storytelling. Classics from this era include the maze-chase game *Pac-Man*, shooter game *Space Invaders*, and platform game *Mario Bros*. *Time* magazine reported that fans spent almost $5 billion on arcade games in 1981, one quarter at a time. That was almost twice what the US film industry earned that year.

With the advent of personal computers, you didn't have to be a computer scientist to play electronic games, but you did need patience to program them on your computer. Dawn Foran started gaming in the early 1980s, when she was five years old. Foran's father would enter pure machine code into their Commodore 64 (C64), a boxy keyboard that hooked up to the Forans' black-and-white TV. Coding this way was a tedious and error-prone typing task. It looks like this: 169 1 160 0 153 0 128 153 0 129 153 130 153 0 131 200 208 241 96. This string of code tells the computer to print the letter *A* one thousand times on the screen.

Because there wasn't much room in the computer's memory, the Forans saved their games on audio cassette tapes. To play these early text games, you typed instructions in response to prompts, displayed as text on the TV screen. Foran said, "We'd take turns playing games in which you were an @ symbol, wander around maps fighting monsters which looked like * and ! Terribly exciting."

In the early 1990s, wider Internet availability spurred the growth of computer games. Fans have played "correspondence" chess by mail for centuries, so naturally the Internet Chess Club started the Internet Chess Server (ICS) in 1992. It was the first time chess players could play via the Internet. ICS displayed the games as text or as ASCII graphics—pictures made of slashes, brackets, and other symbols on a computer keyboard. (ASCII stands for American Standard Code for Information Interchange.) For example, ASCII pawns look like this:

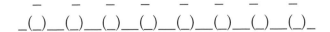

# THE DANGEROUS GAME

A new craze is wasting young people's time, *Scientific American* says. "As there can be no great proficiency in this intricate game without long-continued practice, which demands a great deal of time, no young man who designs to be useful in the world can prosecute it without danger to his best interests." Is this about *Dungeons & Dragons*? Video games? No, this 1859 article was warning against chess, contending that it "robs the mind of valuable time that might be devoted to nobler acquirements, while at the same time it affords no benefit whatever to the body."

Some gamers do find themselves hooked hard on gaming. Founded in 1995, Net Addiction (http://netaddiction.com) offers resources for recovery from problems caused by excessive gaming of any kind. Student and gamer Brianna said, "I'm on the web all the time . . . that's where the music and games and people are, so that's where I am. Everyone knows it's fun, but everyone also knows it can be trouble. You've got to know your limits, and you only know your limits if you do enough to figure them out."

# ROLE-PLAYING GAMES

While video games were moving from computer labs to living rooms, another kind of game was making waves. First released in 1974, *Dungeons & Dragons* (*D&D*) is a tabletop RPG in which players take on the roles of imaginary characters who engage in adventures. Anne Jamison, who writes about fanfiction, compares RPGs to fanfic. "Players already work to develop their characters just to play the game," she said. "The game provides the world and its rules, but the fanfic can kind of weave in and out with the gameplay, so both the story and its source are interactive." Besides creating their own characters, players could invent entirely new settings for the game. (In fact, creators Gary Gygax and Dave Arneson developed the idea out of modifications they made to historical tabletop wargames, similar to *Risk*, in which armies compete to control the world.) *D&D* games inspired players to sketch portraits of their characters and create maps of their new worlds, and a surge of fanworks followed.

*Dungeons & Dragons* players use rule books, dice, and miniature figures (many of them hand-painted) to track their adventures.

Most early *D&D* players met in person, creating bonds that led to lifelong friendships and helped forge a gamer community. Mithen, a gamer who played *D&D* in high school, recalled how her friends Craig and Scott spotted a fellow gamer when a new kid joined their class: "As the teacher droned on, the kid pointed at the teacher and whispered [a *D&D* spell] 'Magic missile.' At which point Craig and Scott knew they'd found a new friend and started talking to him right then and there. Being interested in *D&D* was kind of like a badge at the time, a statement that you were a deliberate outsider." But *D&D* went on to become one of the most popular RPGs of all time and inspired dozens of similar games. It influenced not just fantasy games but the development of open-world video games, in which players can wander freely.

Role-players who wanted to be even closer to the action created a new subculture in the gaming world, live-action role-playing. Instead of playing on a board, like *D&D*, or online, as in *World of Warcraft*, LARPers meet in person to participate in a story world, often using game rules with roots in tabletop RPGs. Some are based on established media sources, such as the Lord of the Rings books or films, while others are set in LARP-specific worlds. It's like participating in a real-life video game or movie that the players cocreate as they go along. As in other areas of fan culture, LARPers seize the opportunity to engage with a story, incorporate art, costumes, and props, and build community.

## PATCHES AND MODS

Like the computer hackers who continued to develop and add to *Spacewar!*, modern gamers patch (alter or modify) games. Often this is encouraged by game developers, who release software allowing fans to design or modify (mod) the skins, or appearance, of their game characters, known as avatars. Developer id Software, for instance, included software to create skins when they released the shooter game *Quake* in 1996. The company had designed only one avatar for the game: a big-muscled, stereotypically male-looking model. Playable female characters were almost unheard of at the time, and id didn't anticipate that players would want to play a female-looking avatar. Using the customization tools, *Quake* fans of all genders developed and shared female skins for the muscular avatars. Their enthusiasm made an impression, and the next versions of *Quake* included a female avatar.

Like fic writers, online game fans exist in a gift economy, freely sharing their game add-ons. A gamer who shared skins online wrote, "Here on this page I shall have some links and some skins that I have made as well as an occasional sampling of my traditional art work. . . . I'm sure you'll find my skins very unique. . . . DOWNLOAD THEM!"

Beyond avatars, gamers may also revise the games themselves. They may modify the game engine, the basic program that controls the game's sound, lighting effects, and other visuals, and the player's movement and navigation through the game world. *Quake* fans, for example, created and shared new levels and even versions of the game with completely different rules.

A patch is an add-on to an existing game program. It changes the original code of a computer game. A patch may fix a problem in a game, add new graphics and sounds, or even completely rework the game. Josephine Starrs and Leon Cmielewski created the game patch Bio Tek Kitchen in 1999. It replaced all the weapons in the game *Marathon* with kitchen utensils. Instead of guns, players are armed with dishcloths, blenders, and spatulas to defend themselves against mutant vegetables running amok in the kitchen lab of a genetic designer.

> **"I AM A GAMER. NOT BECAUSE I DON'T HAVE A LIFE, BUT BECAUSE I CHOOSE TO HAVE MANY."**
> —INTERNET MEME

Gamers enjoy crossovers with other media sources too. Ultimate Simpsons Doom is a mod of the first-person shooter video game *Doom*. Modders Myk Friedman and Walter Stabosz replaced the game's monsters with the family, neighbors, and coworkers of Homer Simpson from the cartoon show *The Simpsons*. The gamer plays as Homer, who is armed with the usual *Doom* weapons but wins Simpsons-specific items such as doughnuts or bowling balls as health-restoring items and bonuses.

In an entirely low-tech way of modding a game character, fan-crafter Nichole knitted tiny Pokémon characters and hid them outside at Pokéstops in Dallas, Texas, where she lives. Pokéstops are locations where players of the mobile game *Pokémon GO* expect to find and catch the digital pocket monsters. She attached tags with her contact info to her knitted monsters, and a parent contacted her to say thank you on behalf of their young daughter, who found a knitted Poliwag. "She was so excited to find a Pokémon at the park," the parent wrote, adding, "My favorite thing, however, is that this experience has motivated [my daughter] to leave 'treasure' at other parks for people as well." Nichole makes her knitting patterns for Pokémon available free online at the fiber-art site Ravelry.com, which hosts many fannish patterns.

# BY GAMERS, FOR GAMERS...
# AND THE WORLD

Game fans mix and match other kinds of fanworks, bringing their perspectives as gamers to the fandom community. In 1998 Jerry Holkins and Mike Krahulik, friends who had played *D&D* (and other games) together in high school, began drawing an online comic strip, or webcomic, called *Penny Arcade*. It followed two guys named Gabe and Tycho who hung around playing and talking about video games. Within two years, it was so popular they quit their jobs to run the comic and associated blog full-time.

When Holkins and Krahulik were growing up, the larger culture stereotyped gamers as oddballs who lived in their parents' basements. Unhappy with the persistent ideas of gamers as uncaring losers and all games as violent, the two gamers founded Child's Play in 2003. The charity organizes gamers to donate children's video games to hospitals and shelters. It also publishes a list of therapeutic video games recommended to help distract children who are in pain, entertain young patients stuck in bed, and relieve kids' sadness, stress, and anxiety. The first year, the organizers planned to collect donations in their garages and distribute them at Christmas. They ended up having to rent a warehouse. After that, supporters donated money instead or ordered games online and shipped them to the charity. In its first fourteen years, Child's Play raised more than $40 million. Krahulik and Holkins were named among *Time*'s 100 Most Influential People in America in 2010. They're credited with fostering a sense of community among geeks and gamers.

Some gamers also design and play games for the greater good. Players of *Foldit*, an online, multiplayer, 3-D puzzle game, are working on solutions to cancer and other diseases. Designed by the Center for Game Science at the University of Washington, the game challenges gamers to tackle the problem of protein folding. Proteins fold up into unique shapes. Discovering their structure is one of the hardest and costliest problems biologists face. It matters because protein folding plays a role in many diseases and also their cures. Since the game's release in 2008, more than 460,000 players from all backgrounds have performed better than the best known computer methods.

In 2011 *Foldit* gamers solved a puzzle that had stumped scientists for fifteen years. They generated a model of a protein that plays a role in the deadly disease AIDS (acquired immunodeficiency syndrome). The scientific journal *Nature* published the results, giving credit to the gamers. The *Foldit* blog said, "This is [a] truly amazing accomplishment. All *Foldit* players should be proud."

## STREAMING GAMEPLAY

From the beginning of electronic games, gamers have recorded themselves playing games, whether to offer strategy and tips or just provide entertainment. Let's Plays (LPs) are videos of one or more people playing and commenting on a video game for the fun of it. They started in 2005 as a series of screenshots with running game commentary on the comedic website *Something Awful* and then moved to YouTube and other video-sharing sites. In video LPs, most of the screen is the gameplay. In a small inset is the gamer playing and commenting on it—usually in a humorous way. Trey Parker, cocreator of *South Park*, said, "I know it might seem weird, especially to those of us from an older generation, that people would spend so much time watching someone else play video games. But I choose to see it as the birth of a new art form."

NoHandsKen is the username of Ken Worrall, a quadriplegic gamer paralyzed from the neck down. He plays with a jouse, a mouth-controlled device that works like a mouse. Worrall plays *Diablo*, *World of Warcraft*, and *StarCraft* on Twitch, a live-streaming video platform for the gaming community. Live-streaming allows viewers to interact with the player, bringing a potentially solitary game experience into a larger community. In a YouTube video called "My Name Is Ken," Worrall credited learning to game with opening up his life after a devastating accident. He wrote on his Twitch, "All the incredible people I've met, talked and played with have had a massive impact on me in a very good way. You guys are amazing."

Fans also record their gameplay and remix it to make new works. Machinima mixes patching and vidding to make a video using the graphics engine of a game. When *World of Warcraft*, for instance, included an option to make characters dance in the game, fans used it to create machinima of the characters dancing to popular music. More unexpectedly, machinima-maker Olanov modified and animated police officers from the violent shooter game *Grand Theft Auto V*. He set them dancing to the cheerful earworm "Happy," a song by Pharrell Williams. In a roundup of machinima made from their games, Rockstar Games featured Olanov's vid, which got more than sixty thousand views on YouTube.

## EMBRACE YOUR WEIRD

Donovan Beltz started gaming when he was very young. He doodled and designed his own game characters on paper, encouraged by his mother and grandmother, who gave him books on how to draw people and anime characters. He recalls, "I started creating characters because it allowed me to use my creative thought process and express myself through digital artwork. It was also a way for me to escape the pain of being bullied, but also allowed me to 'fight back' against the bullies in my imagination [and] to create characters and heroes that I wish I could be, who had courage that I wish I had."

At twenty-four years old, Beltz uses both paper and digital tools, such as Adobe Illustrator and Blender (a 3-D computer graphics program), to design games. He explains, "I'd like to create games that can help kids who are on the autism spectrum (I have Asperger syndrome, a high-functioning form of autism) as well as be able to create games that can be used in everyday situations, such as schools, hospitals, job training, etc."

Felicia Day knows something about being bullied. Day is the creator of the webseries *The Guild*, about a group of MMORPG players, and of the YouTube channel Geek & Sundry, which follows and creates pop and gamer culture. She became the target of cyberbullying during the 2014 Gamergate controversy. Gamergate was a mostly anonymous online harassment campaign organized primarily on Twitter. At their most polite, Gamergate supporters said they objected to growing feminist influence on gaming culture. At their worst, they threatened female gamers with rape and murder.

Day was afraid to speak out at first. In October 2014, however, she wrote a blog post, "The Only Thing I Have to Say about Gamergate." Her peaceful message said, "Games are beautiful, they are creative, they are worlds to immerse yourself in. They are art. And they are worth fighting for, even if the atmosphere is ugly right now. . . . To myself and to everyone else who operates out of love not vengeance: Don't abandon games. Don't cross the street. Gaming needs you. To create, to play, to connect. To represent."

## COMMON GROUND

Fandom mirrors the society in which it exists, with all of its problems. Bao Phi is a Minnesota poet with Vietnamese roots. A self-described nerd of color, when he was a kid, he taught himself to write in Dwarven, the language of Tolkien's dwarves. Even as fandom has become socially acceptable, he's often felt like an outlier among other nerds. "You'd think that fellow nerds, regardless of race and gender," he said, "would give us some humility and common ground to stand on." Too often that is not the case. "Try bringing up issues of race, class, gender, and homophobia on a video game message board and see the vitriolic [vicious] response you get," he continued. "But I think applying a critical mind to the things we like and love is necessary."

Immediately after she posted this, Gamergate cyberbullies doxxed her, or publicly posted her home address (with the implied threat of personal violence). Day closed her comments section. But her message had already reached fans who wanted gaming to remain welcoming.

Former Minnesota Vikings football player Chris Kluwe also wrote an article calling out haters in Gamergate. "I grew up playing games," Kluwe wrote. "I'm sick and tired of the misogynistic [women-hating] culture in today's gaming community." He called for recognition that the game industry has not included and welcomed everyone equally, and celebrated that it is changing. "When people think of 'gamers,'" he said, "I want them to think of . . . athletes who play competitive *League of Legends*, and all the normalization we've accomplished over the years. I want them to think of feminism, and games as an art form—something more than mass entertainment."

Meanwhile, Day stocked her online store with merchandise bearing the slogan Embrace Your Weird. Profits from the sale of the items went to an antibullying charity, Stomp Out Bullying. "Your weirdnesses are your super power," Day said.

# FAN-CREATED GAMES

The video gaming industry earns billions every year, but people can make games for free if they learn some basics. Self-taught game designer Jacob Janerka created prototypes for a game based on the TV show *Stranger Things* (2016– ), which follows a group of kids who search for a friend who has disappeared, seemingly into another dimension. The show's 1980s setting inspired Janerka to mock up a retro-style *Stranger Things* game. He said, "Back then, adventure games were more like text adventures, but it's still that pixel aesthetic that fits in with that kind of time era." He created a few frames of a point-and-click adventure game and posted them as a GIF. The opening frame displays a room from the show. The menu icon looks like one of the walkie-talkies the characters use. The player scrolls a cursor over items in the room to click on options such as Take Pills or Pick up Hammer. Then the scene flickers to the spooky dimension the characters call the Upside Down. Janerka said he had no plans to develop the game.

Game designers don't even need to know how to code to make games. Twine, for instance, is a free, online game-making tool for creating interactive stories and games, similar to choose-your-own-adventure games. The creator writes a passage in a box and then creates different links for the player to choose. The story branches in different directions depending on the player's choices. At their most basic, Twines are all text, but their designers can also add formatting, graphics, and sound. Fans brought their favorites to the gaming table, producing Twines based on everything from the *Odyssey* to *D&D*, *Doctor Who*, and Marvel characters.

Twine is part of a cultural shift toward games that are more about personal experience and less about shooting and fighting. Anna Anthropy has been a champion of such games. In her book *The Rise of the Videogame Zinesters*, she compares Twines to zines, the self-publishing format that opened fandom to a wider audience and enabled its growth. A transgender woman, Anthropy said, "I feel like video games need more voices and more people creating them. . . . And so I absolutely think that queer people and people of color, and people who are outside the nerd status quo need to be involved in making games." With new tools that make game design more accessible, gamers can more easily portray themselves—in their glorious variety—in the medium.

The increase in open-world games, in which players can choose what they want to do, even if it isn't what the designers intended, makes it possible to invent a new game within an old one without any coding at all. In some versions of the super-violent game *Grand Theft Auto (GTA)*, for instance, players can invent their own rules. On the *Fansplaining* podcast episode "Games and Fandom," host Flourish Klink noted that in *GTA*, "you literally can just drive away and explore what else is in the world. There's all these interesting YouTube videos of people who have, like, found a way to drive a car on top of a skyscraper." She continued, "You can just choose to walk away from the things the game is sort of trying to make you do. And go explore the world. . . . And listen to the radio. Drive around the town, listening to the radio. And just have that be your game."

# YOUR GREEN LIGHT

At the heart of fandom is a deep love of stories: hearing, sharing, and participating in them in many ways. Anime USA, an annual con in Washington, DC, describes its weekend-long LARP as "a celebration of fandom and nerdyness that allows you to get into the skin of your favorite character." The 2016 LARP was set on an Earth on the brink of extinction. Alien enemies had banished all adults, and only children remained in the last surviving city. There, one powerful child gathered a resistance to fight for the future. The LARP instructions concluded, "This society of children is your

Warriors clash in the five-day LARP event Battle for Vilegis in Italy. More than twelve hundred players from all over Europe participated in the 2017 event.

base, your headquarters, and your backdrop. It is the only cradle you have left, the last bastion of hope on the planet. "Humanity! BATTLE STATIONS!"

Novelist Doris Lessing described a surprisingly similar scenario in her acceptance speech for the 2007 Nobel Prize in Literature. "Let us suppose our world is ravaged by war," she said, "by the horrors that we all of us easily imagine. . . . It is our stories that will recreate us, when we are torn, hurt, even destroyed. It is the storyteller, the dream-maker, the myth-maker, that is our phoenix, that represents us at our best, and at our most creative."

Strategies and stories, battles and dreams, and humans at their most creative—that's fandom. Fans who participate in fandom are storytellers. Fanfic writers use words. Cosplayers use fabric and fantasy, and visual artists use paint and pixels. Filmmakers and vidders tell stories in moving images. Gamers create, enter into, and share experiences. Even meta is basically a story about a story. Fans who don't make their own fanworks are participants too, for every story needs someone to engage with it.

The 2016 study "Inclusion or Invisibility?" concluded that the entertainment industry needs more decision makers from diverse backgrounds. "It's about who is greenlighting those decisions and who is giving the okay for certain stories to be told," said Stacy L. Smith, one of the authors of the study. While changes at the top of the industry are crucial, fandom has one big advantage: it operates at the grassroots level, without relying on corporate greenlights. On the blog *Black Girl Nerds*, user Sharon recalled writing herself into the story when she was young. "As a Black girl," she said, she wrote fanfiction "to combat the nameless feeling that came over me every time I fell in love with a story that took place in a world where people like me, apparently, didn't exist—or worse, served only as the punchlines or background characters."

Fandom is a world where "people like me" exist, whoever you are. If you can imagine it, write, film, sew, perform, draw, or otherwise participate in it, you can share it, whether online, in person at a con or other gathering, or in a game. Whoever you are and whatever you love, in fandom you are your own green light.

# PEOPLE ON THE INTERNET ARE BEING MEAN

## (MAYBE IT'S EVEN YOU)

Anonymity is crucial for many fans to feel comfortable discussing sensitive or controversial issues online. Anonymity, however, also allows Internet users who would never be so rude in person to say hurtful things online. User Srinitya D commented on a YouTube video, "The internet, which started out as a haven for us socially awkward/ introverted/shy people, has now become a platform for horrid and mean comments . . . it's our duty to actually try and curb this."

The following four guidelines for online behavior are adapted from "Roger's Rules" by media lawyer Roger Dubar. He's also a gamer who founded the multiplayer online game *Nanvaent* in 1991. (It was like *World of Warcraft* with no graphics.) Dubar writes, "Anyone who sends anyone abuse about anything is wrong. . . . That can be illegal. At the very least it's rude."

1. **HUMILITY:** Keep in mind that you might be wrong. The other person might be wrong too. You both might be wrong! Cut yourself and the other person some slack: leave room for humor and apologies.
2. **RESPECT:** Remember the other person has feelings, like you. Imagine you're talking face-to-face. Assume they have good intentions if they say something annoying. Online communications often sound worse than intended.
3. **COMPASSION:** Be kind. You don't know what others are going through. Even if they're being prize-winning jerks, it doesn't hurt you to treat them with courtesy.

**4. CONTEXT:** Consider the circumstances. Is the person joking? A joke is rarely meant to insult you. Even if it is, that's not an excuse to abuse someone else.

## HOW TO DEAL WITH ONLINE BULLIES

If you're playing nice but someone else refuses to, you don't have to put up with it. Everyone has a right to express an opinion, but you don't have to agree or even listen.

1. **DON'T FEED THE TROLLS.** Ignore mean comments, as long as they're minor. They're not about you. They reflect the person who wrote them. Often bullies are acting out of their own insecurities and low self-esteem. They may take any reply as encouragement to keep commenting, so don't give that to them.

2. **TELL SOMEONE ABOUT IT.** Discuss annoying or scary comments with a parent, teacher, or someone you trust. Some online behavior, such as stalking, is illegal and should be reported to the police.

3. **CONSIDER TALKING FACE-TO-FACE.** If the meanness comes from someone you know and if it feels safe, talking to them in person may work better than replying online, where it's easier to be misunderstood. People don't always realize how hurtful they are being online.

4. **BLOCK OR REPORT THE BULLY.** Unfriend, unfollow, screen, or otherwise block all communications from users you don't want. If their behavior is abusive (not just annoying), report it to the site administrator. All social media platforms and phones have these options.

5. **KEEP A RECORD.** Print a hard copy of hostile comments in case you need to show them later.

6. **PROTECT YOUR ONLINE PRIVACY.** Never post your information publicly. Set social media privacy setting to Friends or Friends of Friends. Sites that are open to the public are more likely to receive hostile comments. Create strong passwords, change them regularly, and don't share them.

# GLOSSARY

**alternate universe (AU):** a story that changes the elements of the source material—for example, in a coffee shop, AU characters would be baristas or customers

**anime:** Japanese animation shows

**avatar:** an image that represents a person in a game

**canon:** the official version. Most fans also accept as canon things a creator proclaims about the original work after its release.

**con:** short for "convention," a fan gathering, such as San Diego Comic-Con

**copyright:** the legal right to control an original work. CBS and Paramount hold the copyright to *Star Trek*.

**cosplay:** costume + play, dressing up as a character, such as Sherlock Holmes, or as an item in a story, such as Sherlock Holmes's wallpaper

**crossover:** a mix and match of elements from different fandoms or story worlds, such as Superman meeting Steven Universe

**drabble:** a fanfic either exactly or about one hundred words long

**!:** the punctuation between a characteristic and a name that signals a changed trait. For example, "winged!Harry" is Harry Potter with wings.

**fair use:** the permission US law grants to use copyrighted material under certain conditions

**fan:** a person with a strong interest in or love for a media source, person, or activity. Active fans discuss, perform, and produce their own content inspired by the source. The adjective is *fannish*.

**fan art:** fan-made visual art, including drawing, photography, and digital arts

**fandom:** fan + domain; the community that arises around a media source. Each fandom has its own culture, with rules and expectations. Also, the state of being a fan.

**fan edits:** unofficial changes to an original source, such as a film, that delete, rearrange, or add material to improve or comment on the original

**fanfiction:** fanfic, or fic; fan writings about a media source, fictional or nonfiction (meta), written for love, not money

**fanvids:** or vids; fan-made videos, most commonly short film clips reedited and set to a song to tell a new story. Fans who make vids are vidders.

**fanwork:** the products a fan makes about or in response to that fan's fandom

**filk:** from "fan folk"; a song written by fans for fans, either wholly original or new lyrics set to an existing song

**forum:** a website where users can post public messages, also called a message board

**gamer:** someone who plays games. If you play games, you're a gamer.

**genderbend:** or genderswap; within fandom, changing a character's sex, gender identity, or both from what it is in canon

**GIF:** images presented as a short animation, made with a computer file format called graphics interchange format

**in-universe:** the point of view of fanwork that treats a fictional world as if it were real, called the Game in Sherlock Holmes fandom

**live-action role-playing (LARP):** in-person, in-costume role-playing games

**mashup:** new content made from recombining elements from two or more sources; different from a remix, which is a rearrangement of a single work

**meme:** an idea, catchphrase, image, or piece of information that spreads like a virus, often with small changes

**meta:** nonfiction fanwork about canon or fandom itself, such as commentary on or discussion of a story or character

**modification:** or mod; fan-made changes to a video game that modify its behavior, appearance, or story

**open-world game:** a video game in which the player can wander freely rather than having to stick to a set gameplay

**OTP:** "one true pairing," two characters a fan ships, or pairs romantically. OTPs can be canon (Ron/Hermione) or a fan's favorite ship (Harry/Hermione). A fan's disliked ship is a NOTP or NOtp.

**parody:** a spoof or mockery of another work

**prompt:** an idea for a fanwork, put forth by fans, intended to inspire new content

**racebending:** in the original, negative sense, it's whitewashing, or casting a white actor as a canon character of color. The newer, positive meaning is reimagining a white character as a person of color.

**retcon:** or retroactive continuity; an official revision that adds to or changes a previously established story point, such as making a seemingly childless character a parent

**role-playing game (RPG):** an interactive creative game, such as *Dungeons & Dragons*, played online or in person. Acted out in person, it is LARP (live-action role-playing).

**satire:** works that poke fun of human failings, often through irony, sarcasm, or humor

**science fiction:** also called "sci-fi"; fiction that contains fantastic or extrapolated science themes or elements

**shipping:** portraying or championing a romantic relationship (ship) between characters not (usually) romantically involved in the original source. A shipper is a fan who supports a ship. Ships may be referred to with a combination of the character's names, such as Caryl for Carol + Daryl.

**slash:** fanfic that explores romantic, intimate, or sexual relationships between same-sex characters, usually not together in canon. The name came from the slash mark between Kirk/Spock, the mothership of ships.

**source material:** the canon—the original book, TV show, movie, game, comic, or other text that a fan interacts with

**trope:** a theme or plot gimmick that becomes a staple of fannish storytelling, such as friends who fall in love

**username:** the name a fan uses online or in a video game, also called a handle, nickname, or screen name

**zines:** fan + magazine; self-published and self-distributed printed matter

# SOURCE NOTES

6   Henry Jenkins, "Fandom, Participatory Culture, and Web 2.0," *Confessions of an Aca-Fan*, January 9, 2010, http://henryjenkins.org/2010/01/fandom_participatory _culture_a.html.

6   "FANDOMS," YouTube video, 5:11, posted by Dan Howell, October 12, 2012, https://www.youtube.com/watch?v=oqYkERuoMN8.

6   Aja Romano, "Hamilton Is Fanfic, and Its Historical Critics Are Totally Missing the Point," *Vox*, July 4, 2016, http://www.vox.com/2016/4/14/11418672/hamilton-is -fanfic-not-historically-inaccurate.

7   Ginny Weasley, e-mail to author, June 2, 2016.

8   Kendra James, "Why I Dressed in 'Hamilton' Cosplay for Comic-Con," *Fusion*, July 28, 2016, http://fusion.net/story/331160/hamilton-cosplay-comic-con.

12   Robert McCrum, "The 10 Best First Lines in Fiction," April 28, 2012, https://www .theguardian.com/culture/gallery/2012/apr/29/ten-best-first-lines-fiction.

14   Amy Harmon, "In TV's Dull Summer Days, Plots Take Wing on the Net," *New York Times*, August 19, 1997, http://www.nytimes.com/1997/08/18/business/in-tv-s-dull -summer-days-plots-take-wing-on-the-net.html.

14   Julia Osmon (fan, b. 2002), interview with author, July 1, 2016.

14   Alexandra Alter, "Fantasizing on the Famous," *New York Times*, October 21, 2014, https://www.nytimes.com/2014/10/22/business/media/harry-styles-of-one-direction -stars-in-anna-todds-novel.html.

15   Simon Worrall, "Author Says a Whole Culture—Not a Single 'Homer'—Wrote 'Iliad,' 'Odyssey,'" *National Geographic*, January 3, 2015, http://news.nationalgeographic.com /news/2015/01/150104-homer-iliad-odyssey-greece-book-talk-travel-world.

15   Barry Cunliffe, *Britain Begins* (Oxford: Oxford University Press, 2013), 9.

16   Rudyard Kipling, "The Janeites," *Story-Teller*, May 1924, available online, courtesy of the Rudyard Kipling Society at http://www.telelib.com/authors/K/KiplingRudyard /prose/DebtsandCredits/janeites.html

16   Katie Halsey, *Jane Austen and Her Readers, 1786–1945* (London: Anthem, 2013), 203.

19   Hugo Gernsback, "A New Sort of Magazine," *Amazing Stories*, April 1926, 3, https:// archive.org/stream/AmazingStoriesVolume01Number01#page/n3/mode/2up

19   Camille Bacon-Smith, *Science Fiction Culture* (Philadelphia: University of Pennsylvania Press, 1999), 112.

20   Lisa Pertillar Brevard, *Whoopi Goldberg on Stage and Screen* (Jefferson, NC: McFarland, 2013), 151.

21   "*Star Trek*: Spock, Kirk and Slash Fiction," *Newsweek*, May 4, 2009, http://www .newsweek.com/star-trek-spock-kirk-and-slash-fiction-79807.

21–22  "Newsweek Interview with Shelley Butler," *Fanlore*, November 13, 2013, https://fanlore.org/wiki/Newsweek_Interview_with_Shelley_Butler.

22  "Opening Remarks," *Southern Enclave*, September 1983, 1, http://www.trektales.com/se1_1-28.pdf.

22  Pamela Licalzi O'Connell, "World without End for Fans of Jane Austen," *New York Times*, January 13, 2000, http://www.nytimes.com/2000/01/13/technology/a-world-without-end-for-fans-of-jane-austen.html.

23  Ibid.

23  Grace Bello, "Wattpad Revolutionizes Online Storytelling," *Publisher's Weekly*, December 21, 2012, http://www.publishersweekly.com/pw/by-topic/authors/pw-select/article/55231-pw-select-december-2012-wattpad-revolutionizes-online-storytelling.html.

23  GinnyWeasley, e-mail.

24  Sarah Shaffi, "Rainbow Rowell Speaks Out on Writing Harry Potter Fan Fiction," *Bookseller*, July 16, 2014, http://www.thebookseller.com/news/rainbow-rowell-speaks-out-writing-harry-potter-fan-fiction.

26  Dan Kois, "How One Direction Superfan Anna Todd Went from Waffle House Waitress to Next-Big-Author with Erotic Fan-Fic Series 'After,'" *Billboard*, July 17, 2015, http://www.billboard.com/articles/magazine/6634431/anna-todd-after-one-direction-fan-fiction-book-deal-movie-rights-profile.

26  Ibid.

26  Mithen, e-mail to author, March 20, 2016.

26  Shaffi, "Rainbow Rowell."

27  Mithen (fan), e-mail to author, January 14, 2017.

27  GinnyWeasley, e-mail.

28  *Off Book: Fan Art*, PBS video, 9:39, aired May 3, 2012, http://www.pbs.org/video/2230759496.

28  westoneaststreet, "Jurassic Avatar," *AO3*, January 16, 2017, https://archiveofourown.org/works/6145981.

29  Aja Romano, "Unwrapping Yuletide, the Biggest Fanfiction Event of the Year," *Daily Dot*, December 26, 2013, http://www.dailydot.com/fandom/yuletide-fanfiction-exchange-christmas-2013.

29  "NPR Zombie Spoof: 'Wait Wait Don't Eat Me!,'" *Huffington Post*, May 25, 2011, http://www.huffingtonpost.com/2010/02/03/npr-zombie-spoof-wait-wai_n_447909.html.

29  Helen Joyce, "To Boldly Go . . . ," *1843*, August/September 2016, https://www.1843magazine.com/features/to-boldly-go.

29  Julia Osmon, interview with author, July 1, 2016.

30  Ian Alexander, "The-Fifth-Movement," Tumblr, posted by "lilskeletonprince," March 29, 2017, http://lilskeletonprince.tumblr.com/post/158969504171/the-fifth -movement-cause-of-death-buck-is.

31  John Walker, "The OA's Ian Alexander on His Big Acting Debut and Trans Representation," *Vulture*, December 22, 2016, http://www.vulture.com/2016/12/ the-oa-netflix-ian-alexander-buck.html.

31  NedryOS, "Harry Potter Fanfiction: An Introduction," *Reddit*, February 2015, https://www.reddit.com/r/HPfanfiction/comments/431b2q/harry_potter_ fanfiction_an_updated_introduction.

35  Allan Kohl (teen filmmaker in the 1960s), e-mail to author, January 15, 2017.

35  Ibid.

35  Alison Wickwire, "Believing in Buster," *Comedy*, Summer 1980, 39.

36–37  Francesca Coppa, "Women, Star Trek, and the Early Development of Fannish Vidding," *Transformative Works and Cultures* 1 (2008), http://journal .transformativeworks.org/index.php/twc/article/view/44/64.

38  daisiestdaisy, Tumblr post, May 20, 2014, http://daisiestdaisy.tumblr.com/ post/86330921155/lydiduh-okay-fine-starsky-hutch-has-me [account deactivated].

38  Gary Brolsma, "Who Is Gary Brolsma and What Is the 'Numa Numa Dance'?," GaryBrolsma.com, accessed January 2, 2017, http://www.garybrolsma.com/about -me.

38  Alan Feuer and Jason George, "Internet Fame Is Cruel Mistress for a Dancer of the Numa Numa," *New York Times*, February 26, 2005, http://www.nytimes.com /2005/02/26/nyregion/internet-fame-is-cruel-mistress-for-a-dancer-of-the-numa -numa.html?_r=0.

39  "The Mysterious Ticking Noise," Bella Montoya comment, YouTube, accessed March 9, 2017, https://www.youtube.com/watch?v=Tx1XIm6q4r4.

39  "An Anthropological Introduction to YouTube," YouTube video, 55:33, posted by Michael Wesch, July 26, 2008, https://www.YouTube.com/watch?v=TPAO-lZ4_hU.

39  Ibid.

39  lim (vidder), "How I Made My Vid," December 9, 2007, archived June 20, 2013, https://archive.li/Rzlmf.

40  Milkweedy (vidder), interview with author, January 3, 2017.

40  Ibid.

41  "101 Reasons to Ship Carol + Daryl (The Walking Dead)," YouTube video, 7:02, posted by Athena, November 6, 2014, https://www.youtube.com/ watch?v=VdtCp0ohKyY.

43  Colleen Evanson, "*X-Files* Abridged," summary, Instagram, accessed February 3, 2017, https://www.instagram.com/TheXFilesAbridged.

43 Adywan, *Star Wars Revisited*, accessed February 10, 2017, https://swrevisited.wordpress.com.

44 Jerick, "Hunger Games: Mockingjay 'The Hanging Tree,'" Fanedit.org, April 6, 2016, https://ifdb.fanedit.org/the-hunger-games-mockingjay-the-hanging-tree.

44 Eriq Gardner, "CBS, Paramount Settle Lawsuit over 'Star Trek' Fan Film," *Hollywood Reporter*, January 20, 2017, http://www.hollywoodreporter.com/thr-esq/cbs-paramount-settle-lawsuit-star-trek-fan-film-966433.

44–45 "Fan Films," *Startrek.com*, accessed June 20, 2017, http://www.startrek.com/fan-films.

45 lim, "How I Made My Vid."

47 "Fancy Dress Costumes," *Harper's Bazaar*, 1869, available online at *Victoriana*, accessed January 14, 2017, http://www.victoriana.com/FancyDress/fancydresscostume.htm.

48 Ardern Holt, *Fancy Dresses Described; or, What to Wear at Fancy Balls*, London: Debenham & Freebody/Wyman & Sons, 1887, quoted at Public Domain Review, accessed January 14, 2017, http://publicdomainreview.org/collections/fancy-dresses-described-or-what-to-wear-at-fancy-balls-1887.

49 Forrest James Ackerman, "Out of This World Convention," *Fantastic Universe*, January 1957, Project Gutenberg, accessed January 1, 2017, http://eremita.di.uminho.pt/gutenberg/2/8/5/3/28535/28535-h/28535-h.htm.

49 Luke Plunkett, "Where the Word 'Cosplay' Actually Comes From," *Kotaku*, October 22, 2014, http://kotaku.com/where-the-word-cosplay-actually-comes-from-1649177711.

50 Jane Austen, *Emma*, quoted at Jane Austen Society of North America, February 3, 2017, http://www.jasna.org.

50 Bellexi, Instagram header, accessed January 10, 2017, https://www.instagram.com/bellexi.cosplay.

52–53 Keelin, communication with author, March 4, 2017.

53 Marjorie Cohee Manifold, "Enchanting Tales and Imagic Stories: The Educational Benefits of Fanart Making," *Art Education*, November 2013, 12.

55 Chaka Cumberbatch, "I'm a Black Female Cosplayer and Some People Hate It," *xoJane*, February 4, 2013, http://www.xojane.com/issues/mad-back-cosplayer-chaka-cumberbatch.

55 Ibid.

56 Shawn Taylor, "Silicon Valley Comic Con: Report Back," *Nerds of Color*, March 20, 2016, https://thenerdsofcolor.org/2016/03/20/silicon-valley-comic-con-report-back/#more-19848.

57 Aria Baci, "Interview with Dax ExclamationPoint," *Geeks Out*, March 14, 2016, http://geeksout.org/blogs/aria-baci/interview-dax-exclamationpoint.

57   Heather Henley, "Savannah Drag Queen Dax Exclamationpoint Joining 'RuPaul's Drag Race' This Season," *Do Savannah*, February 2, 2016, http://www.dosavannah .com/article/tue-02022016-0210/savannah-drag-queen-dax-exclamationpoint -joining-rupaul-s-drag-race-season.

57–58   Monica Hunasikatti, "Hijabi Hooligan Cosplay: I Can Still Have Fun without Compromising My Faith!," *Black Nerd Problems*, October 17, 2016, http:// blacknerdproblems.com/hijabi-hooligan-cosplay-i-can-still-have-fun-without -compromising-my-faith.

58   Breeanna Hare, "Peter Griffin from 'Family Guy,' in Real Life," *CNN*, January 8, 2015, http://www.cnn.com/2015/01/08/showbiz/feat-peter-griffin-family-guy-real -life.

58   Samantha Albala, "'Cosplay Is Not Consent' at the New York Comic Con," *Bust*, October 13, 2014, http://bust.com/feminism/13137-consent-and-feminism-at-the -new-york-comic-con.html.

59   Edie Nugent, "Cosplay Is, of Course, Good for Your Health," *Geek & Sundry*, March 9, 2016, http://geekandsundry.com/beyond-dress-up-how-cosplay-is -good-for-your-health.

59   Ibid.

59   Victoria Hardt, quoted in Edie Nugent, "Cosplay, Good for Your Health."

59–60   Jonathan Hernandez, "Marvel Fandom Feature: Cosplay Parents," *Marvel Report*, July 14, 2016, http://themarvelreport.com/2016/07/marvel-fandom-feature -cosplay-parents.

60   "Anti-Harassment Policy," New York Comic Con, accessed April 19, 2017, http:// www.newyorkcomiccon.com/About/Harassment-Policy.

61   Molly McArdle, "This Is How *Star Trek* Invented Fandom," *GQ*, September 21, 2016, http://www.gq.com/story/this-is-how-star-trek-invented-fandom.

62   Brad O'Farrell, *Off Book*: "Fan Art!," PBS video, 9:39, at 0:43, aired May 3, 2012, http://www.pbs.org/video/off-book-fan-art-creativity/.

63   Bryan Konietzko, Tumblr post, March 30, 2013, http://bryankonietzko.tumblr .com/post/46687253373/i-remember-back-in-the-avatar-days-the-typical.

64   Jonathan Jones, "Contemporary Art Isn't Original—Even Copying Has Been Done Before," *Guardian* (US ed.), May 30, 2014, https://www.theguardian.com /commentisfree/2014/may/30/contemporary-art-isnt-original-marina-abramovic -row.

64   Umberto Eco, "Vegetal and Mineral Memory: The Future of Books," Bibliotecha Alexandrina, November 20–26, 2003, http://www.umbertoeco.com/en/bibliotheca- alexandrina-2003.html.

66–67   Clive Thompson, "When Copy and Paste Reigned in the Age of Scrapbooking," *Smithsonian*, July 2014, http://www.smithsonianmag.com/history/when-copy-and -paste-reigned-age-scrapbooking-180951844.

67 Maegan Tintari, "My Grandma's Personal Scrapbooks of Hollywood Movie Stars from the 1930s," . . . *loveMaegan.com*, March 15, 2011, http://www.lovemaegan .com/2011/03/my-grandmas-personal-scrapbooks-of-hollywood-movie-stars-from -the-1930s-vintage-books.html.

68–69 "Interview with Rebecca Sugar, Creator of Steven Universe," *Animac*, April 22, 2015, http://www.animac.cat/magazine_en/entrevista-amb-rebecca-sugar-creadora -de-steven-universe.

69 Evan Narcisse, "Race, Sci-Fi, and Comics: A Talk with Dwayne McDuffie," *Atlantic*, March 5, 2010, http://www.theatlantic.com/entertainment/archive/2010/03/race -sci-fi-and-comics-a-talk-with-dwayne-mcduffie/37063.

69–70 Margalit Fox, "Dwayne McDuffie, Comic-Book Writer, Dies at 49," *New York Times*, February 23, 2011, http://www.nytimes.com/2011/02/24/arts/design /24mcduffie.html.

70 Evan Narcisse, "Come On, Video Games, Let's See Some Black People I'm Not Embarrassed By," *Kotaku*, March 29, 2012, http://kotaku.com/5897227/come-on -video-games-lets-see-some-black-people-im-not-embarrassed-by.

71 "What Is 'Racebending'?" *Racebending*, accessed March 5, 2017, http://racebending .tumblr.com/what-is-racebending.

71 Sarah Holmes, "Having Hermione Look Like Me Is Amazing," *BBC News*, December 23, 2015, http://www.bbc.com/news/world-us-canada-35156893.

72 "The Council of Elrond," *Lord of the Rings: The Fellowship of the Ring* (Extended Edition), directed by Peter Jackson (2001; Burbank, CA: New Line Home Entertainment, 2002), DVD.

72–73 Jennifer Izykowski, "We Delve into the World of 'Fan Art', Conventions, and More in Our Interview with Talented Artist Ashlee Casey," *Nerd Recites*, July 7, 2016, http://thenerdrecites.com/we-delve-into-the-world-of-fan-art-conventions-and -more-in-our-depth-interview-with-talented-artist-ashlee-casey-2417.

73 Binkk7 (fan artist), communication with author, March 19, 2017.

73 Binkk7 (fan artist), interview with author, March 9, 2017.

74 Jetsonarama, "An Introduction to Debra Yepa-Pappan from Chip Thomas," *Vandalog* (blog), March 27, 2014, https://blog.vandalog.com/2014/03/an -introduction-to-debra-yepa-pappan-from-chip-thomas.

75 "Star Wars Collage Fan Art," *Geek x Girls*, June 3, 2016, http://geekxgirls.com /article.php?ID=7133.

75 Melissa Moffat, "Melissa Moffat: An Interview by Dario Rutigliano," *LandEscape Art Review*, July 25, 2015, 33, https://issuu.com/landescapeartpress/docs/landescape_art _review_-_anniversary_0a5396b85a1a36/22.

75 Mycks, "About Mycks Art Studio," Mycks Art Studio, accessed March 19, 2017, https://www.amazon.com/handmade/Mycks-Art-Studio.

76 Amy Ratcliffe, "Fan Art Friday #94—It's Time for InkTober," *Nerdist*, October 14, 2016, http://nerdist.com/fan-art-friday-94-inktober-october-halloween/.

79  Matthew Price "Online Program 'The Guild' to Debut in Comic Book Series," *News OK*, October 2, 2009, http://newsok.com/article/3405469.

79  *Welcome to Night Vale*, accessed January 14, 2017, http://www.welcometonightvale.com.

79  Toril Orlesky, "Because All of Us Are Normal!," *Starlock*, accessed June 20, 2017, http://14180.work/image/56161860881.

79  Daniel Durrant, "Interview with Two Comic Con Legends," *Copic*, July 14, 2016, https://imaginationinternationalinc.com/copic/inspire/showcase/interview-two-comic-con-legends.

81  Jonathan Malcolm Lampley, "Afterword: The Past and Future of Fandom Studies," in *Fan CULTure: Essays on Participatory Fandom in the 21st Century*, ed. Kristin M. Barton and Jonathan Malcolm Lampley (Jefferson, NC: McFarland, 2013), 194–95.

82  Maria Bustillos, "On Video Games and Storytelling: An Interview with Tom Bissell," *New Yorker*, March 19, 2013, http://www.newyorker.com/books/page-turner/on-video-games-and-storytelling-an-interview-with-tom-bissell.

84  Stewart Brand, "SPACEWAR: Fanatic Life and Symbolic Death among the Computer Bums," *Rolling Stone*, December 7, 1972, http://www.wheels.org/spacewar/stone/rolling_stone.html.

84  Ibid.

85  Dawn Foran, "Select Hero or Heroine," in *Chicks Dig Gaming* (Des Moines: Mad Norwegian, 2014), 23.

86  "Chess Playing Excitement," in *Scientific American*, vol. 1 (New York: Munn, 1859), 9, https://books.google.com/books?id=90hGAQAAIAAJ&dq, Google edition.

86  Bronwyn T. Williams, *Shimmering Literacies* (New York: Peter Lang, 2009), 189.

86  Denny S. Bryce, "Must-Read Fan Fiction from 'The Hunger Games,' Anime/Manga, Jane Austen and More," *USA Today*, March 15, 2017, http://happyeverafter.usatoday.com/2017/03/15/denny-s-bryce-fan-fiction-recs-hunger-games-anime-manga-jane-austen/.

87  Mithen, e-mail to author, January 14, 2017.

88  Anne-Marie Schleiner, "Parasitic Interventions: Game Patches and Hacker Art," Opensorcery.net, August 1999, http://opensorcery.net/patchnew.html.

89  Luke Plunkett, "Artist Is Hiding Tiny Pokémon around Pokéstops," *Kotaku*, August 12, 2016, http://kotaku.com/artist-is-hiding-tiny-pokemon-around-pokestops-1785180454.

91  Matt Peckham, "Foldit Gamers Solve AIDS Puzzle That Baffled Scientists for a Decade," *Time*, September 19, 2011, http://techland.time.com/2011/09/19/foldit-gamers-solve-aids-puzzle-that-baffled-scientists-for-decade.

91  Trey Parker, "Felix Kjellberg (a.k.a. PewDiePie)," *Time*, April 20, 2016, http://time.com/4302406/felix-kjellberg-pewdiepie-2016-time-100.

92 NoHandsKen, Twitch, accessed January 22, 2017, https://www.twitch.tv/nohandsken.

92 Donovan Beltz, e-mail to author, January 30, 2017.

92–93 Ibid.

93 Felicia Day, "The Only Thing I Have to Say about Gamergate," *Felicia's Melange*, October 2014, http://thisfeliciaday.tumblr.com/post/100700417809/the-only-thing-i-have-to-say-about-gamer-gate.

93 caphebaophi (Bao Phi), "NOCs (Nerds of Color)," Minneapolis Star Tribune, January 20, 2010, http://www.startribune.com/nocs-nerds-of-color/82188702.

94 Chris Kluwe, "Why #Gamergaters Piss Me the F*** Off," *Cauldron*, October 21, 2014, https://the-cauldron.com/why-gamergaters-piss-me-the-f-off-a7e4c7f6d8a6#.crhfah4ss.

94 Felicia Day, "Felicia Day 'Embrace Your Weird' Apparel," *Represent*, accessed January 22, 2017, https://represent.com/felicia/day-embrace-your-weird-charity-campaign.

94 Jacob Janerka, quoted in W. Harry Fortuna, "A 'Stranger Things' Game in Classic LucasArts Style? Yes Please," *Inverse*, August 2, 2016, https://www.inverse.com/article/19002-stranger-things-pixel-game.

95 Cara Ellison, "Anna Anthropy and the Twine Revolution," *Guardian* (US ed.), April 10, 2013, https://www.theguardian.com/technology/gamesblog/2013/apr/10/anna-anthropy-twine-revolution

95–96 Flourish Klink, "Transcript: Episode 30: Games and Fandom," *Fansplaining*, September 9, 2016, http://fansplaining.com/post/150176819728/transcript-episode-30-games-and-fandom.

96–97 "LARP (Live Action Role-Playing)," *Anime USA*, accessed February 3, 2017, http://animeusa.org/larp.

97 Doris Lessing, "The Nobel Lecture Prize in Literature 2007," Nobel Prize, December 7, 2007, http://nobelprize.org/nobel_prizes/literature/laureates/2007/lessing-lecture_en.html.

97 Eric Deggans, "Hollywood Has a Major Diversity Problem, USC Study Finds," *NPR*, February 22, 2016, http://www.npr.org/sections/thetwo-way/2016/02/22/467665890/hollywood-has-a-major-diversity-problem-usc-study-finds.

97 Sharon, "My Love Letter to Fanfiction," *Black Girl Nerds*, February 25, 2015, https://blackgirlnerds.com/love-letter-fanfiction-fanfiction-turducken-literature-lot-important-woc-probably-think.

98 "The Internet Takeover #NicerInternet Special," Srinitya D comment, April 26, YouTube, 2016, February 16, 2015, https://www.youtube.com/watch?v=dq6u27Ul5CU.

98 Roger Dubar, "Roger's Rules for Online Behaviour," *Huffington Post* (UK), February 5, 2016, http://www.huffingtonpost.co.uk/roger-dubar/rules-for-online-behaviour_b_9804340.html.

# SELECTED BIBLIOGRAPHY

Alexander, Leigh. "The Joy of Text: The Fall and Rise of Interactive Fiction." *Guardian* (US ed.), October 22, 2014. http://www.theguardian.com/technology/2014/oct/22/interactive-fiction-awards-games.

Anthropy, Anna. *Rise of the Videogame Zinesters: How Freaks, Normals, Amateurs, Artists, Dreamers, Dropouts, Queers, Housewives, and People Like You Are Taking Back an Art Form*. New York: Seven Stories, 2012.

Bacon-Smith, Camille. *Enterprising Women: Television Fandom and the Creation of Popular Myth*. Philadelphia: University of Pennsylvania Press, 1992.

Bartlett, Jamie. "4chan: The Role of Anonymity in the Meme-Generating Cesspool of the Web." *Wired*, October 1, 2013. http://www.wired.co.uk/article/4chan-happy-birthday.

Barton, Kristin M., and Jonathan Malcolm Lampley, eds. *Fan CULTure: Essays on Participatory Fandom in the 21st Century*. Jefferson, NC: McFarland, 2013.

Bissell, Tom. *Extra Lives: Why Video Games Matter*. New York: Pantheon, 2010.

Bogost, Ian. *How to Talk about Videogames*. Minneapolis: University of Minnesota Press, 2015.

boyd, danah. *It's Complicated: The Social Lives of Networked Teens*. New Haven, CT: Yale University Press, 2014.

Brozek, Jennifer, Robert Smith?, and Lars Pearson, eds. *Chicks Dig Gaming*. Des Moines: Mad Norwegian, 2014.

Delwiche, Aaron, and Jennifer Jacobs Henderson, eds. *The Participatory Cultures Handbook*. New York: Routledge, 2013.

Doctorow, Cory. "Creativity vs. Copyright." In *The Great Big Beautiful Tomorrow*. Oakland: PM, 2011. Available online under a Creative Commons Attribution-NonCommercial-ShareAlike 3.0 license at http://craphound.com/gbbt/download.

Duffett, Mark. *Understanding Fandom: An Introduction to the Study of Media Fan Culture*. New York: Bloomsbury Academic, 2013.

Erzen, Tanya. *Fanpire: The Twilight Saga and the Women Who Love It*. Boston: Beacon, 2012.

"FANDOMS." YouTube video, 5:11. Posted by Dan Howell, October 12, 2012. https://www.youtube.com/watch?v=oqYkERuoMN8.

Goldberg, Daniel, and Linus Larsson, eds. *State of Play: Sixteen Voices on Video Games*. New York: Seven Stories, 2015.

Gray, Jonathan, Cornel Sandvoss, and C. Lee Harrington, eds. *Fandom: Identities and Communities in a Mediated World*. New York: NYU Press, 2007.

Hellekson, Karen, ed. *Fan Fiction and Fan Communities in the Age of the Internet: New Essays*. Jefferson NC: McFarland, 2006.

Holt, Ardern. *Fancy Dresses Described: or, What to Wear at Fancy Balls*. London: Debenham & Freebody/Wyman & Sons, 1887. Available online at https://archive.org/details/fancydressesdesc00holtrich.

Jamison, Anne. *Fic: Why Fanfiction Is Taking Over the World*. Dallas: Smart Pop, 2013.

Jenkins, Henry. *Convergence Culture: Where Old and New Media Collide*. New York: NYU Press, 2006.

———. *Textual Poachers: Television Fans and Participatory Culture*. 2nd ed. New York: Routledge, 2012.

Jenkins, Henry, Mizuko Ito, and danah boyd. *Participatory Culture in a Networked Era: A Conversation on Youth, Learning, Commerce, and Politics*. Boston: Polity, 2015.

Johnson, Claudia L. "Austen Cults and Cultures." In *The Cambridge Companion to Jane Austen*. Edited by Edward Copeland and Juliet McMaster. Cambridge: Cambridge University Press, 1997, 243–44.

Johnson, Steven. *Everything Bad Is Good for You: How Today's Popular Culture Is Actually Making Us Smarter*. New York: Riverhead, 2005.

Kinsella, Felicity. "The All-Consuming Phenomenon of Teen Girl Fandom." *i-D*, June 11, 2015. https://i-d.vice.com/en_gb/article/the-all-consuming-phenomenon-of-teen-girl-fandom.

Larsen, Katherine, and Lynn Zubernis. *Fan Culture: Theory/Practice*. Newcastle Upon Tyne, UK: Cambridge Scholars, 2012.

Levi, Antonia. *Samurai from Outer Space: Understanding Japanese Animation*. Chicago: Open Court, 1996.

Manifold, Marjorie Cohee. "Enchanting Tales and Imagic Stories: The Educational Benefits of Fanart Making." *Art Education*, November 2013, 12–19.

Phi, Bao. "NOCs (Nerds of Color)." *Minneapolis Star Tribune*, January 20, 2010. http://www.startribune.com/nocs-nerds-of-color/82188702.

Pugh, Sheenagh. *The Democratic Genre: Fan Fiction in a Literary Context*. Brigend, Wales: Seren, 2005.

Reid, Calvin. "S&S Acquires Anna Todd's 'After' Series from Wattpad." *Publisher's Weekly*, May 27, 2014. http://www.publishersweekly.com/pw/by-topic/industry-news/book-deals/article/62475-s-s-acquires-anna-todd-s-after-series-from-wattpad.html.

Ross, Sharon Marie, and Louisa Ellen Stein, eds. *Teen Television: Essays on Programming and Fandom*. Jefferson, NC: McFarland, 2008.

Stein, Louisa Ellen. *Millennial Fandom: Television Audiences in a Transmedia Age*. Iowa City: University of Iowa Press, 2015.

Sutherland, Kathryn. "Jane Austen's Juvenilia." *British Library Newsletter*. Accessed January 2, 2017. http://www.bl.uk/romantics-and-victorians/articles/jane-austens-juvenilia.

Williams, Bronwyn T. *Shimmering Literacies*. New York: Peter Lang, 2009.

# FURTHER READING, VIEWING, AND WEBSITES

## BOOKS

Ashcraft, Brian, and Luke Plunkett. *Cosplay World*. New York: Prestel, 2014. The book includes photographs of cosplay from the 1970s onward and short interviews with fifty-eight people involved with cosplay, including historians, cosplayers, writers, website creators, teachers, and makers.

Brothers, Megan. *Weird Girl and What's His Name*. New York: Three Rooms, 2015. This young adult novel is about Rory and Lula, high school geeks who share a love of movies and the *X-Files*. They find friendship through fandom and explore sexuality in an isolating world.

Coppa, Francesca. *The Fanfiction Reader: Folk Tales for the Digital Age*. Ann Arbor: University of Michigan Press, 2017. Coppa's collection of fanfic from fandoms includes *Star Trek*, *Star Wars*, *Doctor Who*, and others, and is accompanied by short essays.

Day, Felicia. *You're Never Weird on the Internet (Almost): A Memoir*. New York: Touchstone, 2015. Day's amusing and informative memoir of growing up weird by the creator of the first YouTube serial, the *Guild*, is based on her experience as an avid player of *World of Warcraft*.

Howell, Dan, and Phil Lester. *The Amazing Book Is Not on Fire: The World of Dan and Phil*. New York: Random House Books for Young Readers, 2015. This book looks into the world of Dan (danisnotonfire) and Phil (AmazingPhil), two awkward video bloggers who share their lives with millions of subscribers on YouTube.

Hurley, Kameron. *The Geek Feminist Revolution*. New York: Tor, 2016. A collection of essays by an award-winning sci-fi author and blogger, the book addresses ongoing conversations in the geek community, including the role of women.

Kaplan, Arie. *The Wild World of Gaming Culture*. Minneapolis: Lerner, 2014. Dive into the many ways gamers take their enthusiasm beyond the screen.

Langley, Alex. *The Geek Handbook: Practical Skills and Advice for the Likable Modern Geek*. Iola, WI: Krause, 2012. This handbook features a collection of articles and lists about geekery, including cool gadgets and essential movies and TV, overcoming social anxieties, making friends, dating, and much more.

Maggs, Sam. *The Fangirl's Guide to the Galaxy: A Handbook for Girl Geeks*. Philadelphia: Quirk, 2015. Maggs offers tips on "geek culture and how it intersects with being a lady," including how to make nerdy friends, attend conventions, rock awesome cosplay, write fanfic, defeat Internet trolls, and generally be a strong female character.

Moskowitz, Hannah, and Kat Helgeson. *Gena/Finn*. San Francisco: Chronicle Books, 2016. This young adult novel is told entirely in texts, chats, and blog posts between Gena, a fanfic writer, and mutual fan Finn. As their friendship develops, neither one expects the drama that unfolds.

Rowell, Rainbow. *Fangirl: A Novel*. New York: St. Martin's Griffin, 2013. *Fangirl* is a novel about Cath, author of a popular fanfic about boy wizard Simon Snow, who finds herself unsure about how to integrate her online life into her new life at college. Rowell published a companion novel about Simon Snow, *Carry On*, in 2015.

Segal, Stephen H., ed. *Geek Wisdom: The Sacred Teachings of Nerd Culture*. Philadelphia: Quirk, 2011. Who said, "I've got a bad feeling about this"? Learn the source of this question and about two hundred other oft-quoted sayings from pop culture. (Answer, from p. 134: Han Solo first said he had a bad feeling in *Star Wars* [1977]. By *Return of the Jedi* [1983], it had become a "really bad" feeling.)

Thorsson, Shawn. *Make: Props and Costume Armor: Create Realistic Science Fiction & Fantasy Weapons, Armor, and Accessories*. San Francisco: Maker Media, 2016. A master prop maker offers tips for creating amazing cosplay costumes and props with simple tools and materials mostly available at a hardware or office supply store.

Tregay, Sarah. *Fan Art*. New York: Katherine Tegen Books, 2014. In this young adult novel, Jamie, a high schooler, fears that if his best friend Mason found out he was gay—let alone in love with him—Mason would never speak to him again. Then a short comic in the school paper about two boys falling in love changes everything.

Triggs, Teal. *Fanzines: The DIY Revolution*. San Francisco: Chronicle Books, 2010. Triggs presents a history of fanzines, from early handmade publications of sci-fi communities of the 1930s to the e-zine scene in the Internet age, with hundreds of images.

Weldon, Glen. *The Caped Crusade: Batman and the Rise of Nerd Culture*. New York: Simon & Schuster, 2016. Weldon's cultural history of Batman, with his obsession with gadgets, single-mindedness, and lack of superhuman powers, reflects the rise of modern geek culture.

## VIDEOS AND FILMS

"All Creative Work Is Derivative." YouTube video, 2:20. Posted by Question Copyright. February 9, 2010. https://www.youtube.com/watch?v=jcvd5JZkUXY.
This video, by Nina Paley, animates photographs of artwork from around the world and throughout time to show the similarities among creative works. The video was taken at the Metropolitan Museum of Art, New York City.

"A Fair(y) Use Tale." Center for Internet and Society video, 10:14. Posted by the Documentary Film Program, March 1, 2007. http://cyberlaw.stanford.edu/blog/2007/03/fairy-use-tale.
Professor Eric Faden of Bucknell University created this funny overview of US copyright law and fair use. Using film clips of just a few seconds long, he delivers the message through the words of Disney characters.

"Incredible Fanvid Compresses Decades of Fandom into 5 Minutes." Tor, August 14, 2012. http://www.tor.com/2012/08/14/incredible-fanvid-compresses-decades-of-fandom-into-5-minutes.

This article features a fanvid "We Didn't Start the Fire" (set to a song by Billy Joel) by vidders fiercynn and scribe that conveys the history of fandom. The password to view this vid is fandom! (with the exclamation point).

"'I Ship It'—an Icona Pop Parody." YouTube video, 3:03. Posted by Not Literally Productions, November 20, 2013. https://www.youtube.com/watch?v=LCDgJiPBxfI.

This song about shipping characters includes ones who may not even be in the same universe, such as Captain Kirk + Princess Leia, or BBC's Sherlock/the Doctor (Doctor Who).

"Numa, Numa." YouTube video, 1:39. Posted by "Dork Daily," December 11, 2006. https://www.youtube.com/watch?v=KmtzQCSh6xk.

This is the original, digitally remastered, of the first viral video, by Gary Brolsma. For more information, check out http://www.garybrolsma.com.

Off Book
https://www.YouTube.com/user/PBSoffbook

Off Book is a PBS web series of short videos that explores Internet culture and the people that create it. Topics include tattoos, 3-D printing, indie games, animated GIFs, cosplay, fan art, and more.

*Trekkies.* DVD. Directed by Roger Nygard. Hollywood, CA: Paramount Pictures, 1997.

Denise Crosby, who portrayed Tasha Yar in *Star Trek: The Next Generation*, interviews *Star Trek* fans and cast members about how the show affected their lives.

"Us | Multifandom." YouTube video, 3:55. Posted by "lim," June 2, 2007. https://www.youtube.com/watch?v=_yxHKgQyGx0.

A labor of love about fandom itself, this multifandom metavid drew a lot of nonfan attention to fanvids and fandom.

*Web Junkie.* DVD. Directed by Shosh Shlam and Hilla Medalia. New York: Alive Mind Cinema, 2013.

China declared Internet addiction a clinical disorder. Filmmakers Shlam and Medalia filmed inside one of China's controversial rehab camps for teenagers deemed to be addicted and in need of deprogramming.

## WEBSITES

*Black Nerd Problems*
http://blacknerdproblems.com

A team of writers of color consider race representation in geek culture, discussing such things as why there are almost no people of color in the Hobbit films. The writers share their love for science fiction, fantasy, comics, and more.

*Confessions of an Aca-Fan, the Official Weblog of Henry Jenkins*
http://henryjenkins.org
*Aca-fan* is short for *academic* + *fan*, and the blog of Professor Jenkins is bursting full of fascinating fannish info, interviews, and ideas. Jenkins is a pioneer in the field of media and fandom studies, and a prolific blogger and writer. The first of his many books is the groundbreaking look at fandom, *Textual Poachers: Television Fans and Participatory Culture*.

"Copyright and Fair Use": Stanford University Libraries
http://fairuse.stanford.edu
The site includes sections on copyright FAQs, an introduction to permissions, website permissions, academic and educational permissions, the public domain, fair use, releases, and copyright research.

Cosplay Tutorial: A Resource for Costumers
http://cosplaytutorial.com
Instructions are given about everything from making armor to wearing wigs to using a 3-D printer. The site also includes lots of helpful cosplay tips, such as suggesting cosplayers hide their weapons in garbage bags when in public to avoid freaking people out.

*Daily Dot*
http://www.dailydot.com
With its slogan "Your Internet. Your News" the *Daily Dot* calls itself "the ultimate destination for original reporting on Internet culture and life online." It reports on a wide range of topics related to fandom. Along with its professional staff, young writers contribute regularly from around the globe.

DeviantArt
http://www.deviantart.com
Founded in 2000, DeviantArt has more than thirty-eight million registered users, making it the largest online social network for artists and art enthusiasts. It is a platform for fan (and nonfan) artists to upload, promote, and share their works.

*Fandom*
http://fandom.wikia.com
*Fandom* hosts pop culture news and fan-created encyclopedias (wikis) for game, film, TV, and other media properties. Hundreds of thousands of communities host information, news, and speculation on their favorite works.

*Fan/Fic* Magazine
https://fanslashfic.com
*Fan/Fic* is an online magazine for fanfic readers and writers. The magazine includes articles and personal essays about fandom culture, practical advice on how to make crafts, and interviews with people in the community. Recommended: Read the three-part article, "Beginner's Guide to Creating Fanart," by Jae Bailey, April 28, 2016.

*Fansplaining*
http://fansplaining.com
The audio podcast by, about, and for fandom features interviews with fans and professionals who are also fans, hosted by Flourish Klink and Elizabeth Minkel. Written transcripts of episodes are available too.

*Geek & Sundry*
http://www.geekandsundry.com
*Geek & Sundry* is a website and a YouTube channel that brings together fans from all over the world who love games and all counterculture fannish things.

Know Your Meme
http://knowyourmeme.com
The website is dedicated to documenting Internet phenomena: viral videos, image macros, catchphrases, web celebs, and more. Any registered member can submit a meme or viral phenomena. The editorial staff also provides interviews or Q&As with subjects of memes or notable individuals in the meme culture.

*Kotaku*
http://kotaku.com
The video game website and blog covers all aspects of gaming, including cosplay, game design, news, and culture. *Kotaku* states that it is for gamers of all ethnicities, genders, and sexual orientations.

Latinx Geeks
http://latinxgeeks.com
A community for Latinx who love all things geeky and nerdy, Latinx Geeks celebrates and brings attention to the need for positive Latinx representation in movies, comic books, television, and games.

Learn to Code with Me
http://learntocodewith.me/posts/code-for-free
This site lists forty-five free online resources to learn computer code to build games, websites, and more. The list includes codeacademy.com, which offers step-by-step tutorials.

*The Mary Sue*
http://www.themarysue.com
A site that covers geek culture, *The Mary Sue* reports on comic books, movies, genre television, space exploration, emerging technologies, video games, and the weirdest finds on the Internet. The community prides itself on being passionate, inclusive, and feminist.

*Nerdist*
http://nerdist.com
With daily news and reviews of the latest games, movies, and comics, *Nerdist*'s team of writers explores the nerd fabric of the pop-culture landscape. Home to the Nerdist Podcast Network, Nerdist News, and Nerdist Presents, *Nerdist* was started by comedian and pop culture commentator Chris Hardwick.

*The Nerds of Color*
https://www.thenerdsofcolor.org
This community of fans loves superheroes, sci-fi, fantasy, and video games and looks at nerd/geek fandom with a culturally critical eye.

Organization for Transformative Works (OTW)

http://www.transformativeworks.org

Designed, run, and wholly supported by fans, the OTW is a major platform for fanworks and fan activism. It hosts fanfiction at *Archive of Our Own (AO3)*; a fandom wiki. Fanlore; *Transformative Works and Cultures*, a peer-reviewed academic journal; and more.

Racebending

http://www.racebending.com

Racebending.com is an international grassroots organization of media consumers that advocates for underrepresented groups in entertainment media. The site is dedicated to furthering equal opportunities in Hollywood and beyond.

*TV Tropes*

http://tvtropes.org

Calling itself the All-Devouring Pop-Culture Wiki, *TV Tropes* collects, catalogs, and amply describes tropes, or storytelling devices, from across all media and fandoms. The site is fun to read.

Wattpad: Fanfiction

https://www.wattpad.com/stories/fanfiction

Wattpad is a social network and platform for storytelling, designed for mobile devices. A major site for fanfiction, it also hosts nonfic writing.

*Worship the Fandom*

http://www.worshipthefandom.com

This site, "where creativity and fan culture converge," hosts user-generated fan content, including fan art, fanfiction, cosplay, fashion, food, and cons.

# INDEX

# ABOUT THE AUTHOR

Francesca Davis DiPiazza is an author and editor—and a fan. She endured a pre-Internet childhood by watching reruns of the original *Star Trek*. Sharing her fanworks online has since connected her to other fans worldwide. In addition to creating fic and vids in different fandoms, she writes award-winning nonfiction, including *Friend Me! Six Hundred Years of Social Networking in America*, an investigation of the history of socializing.

# PHOTO ACKNOWLEDGMENTS

The images in this book are used with the permission of: Theo WargoGetty Images Entertainment/Getty Images, p. 5; iStock.com/skyNext, p. 13; The Advertising Archives/Alamy Stock Photo, p. 17; Wikimedia Commons (public domain), p. 18; Christophe Meireis/Starface/Polaris/Newscom, p. 25;© JoJo Whilden/Netflix/Kobal/REX/Shutterstock, p. 31; © Todd Strand/Independent Picture Service, p. 33; Photo courtesy Allan T. Kohl., p. 35; Yermia Riezky Santiago/Alamy Stock Photo, p. 42; Chronicle/Alamy Stock Photo, p. 47; Charles Frattini/NY Daily News Archive/Getty Images, p. 49; © Lindsey Owens/Independent Picture Service, p. 51; Veronica Bruno/Alamy Stock Photo, p. 52; Manan VATSYAYANA/AFP PHOTO/Getty Images, p. 56; Michael Preston/Alamy Stock Photo, p. 61; All Canada Photos/Alamy Stock Photo, p. 63; Paul Fearn/Alamy Stock Photo, p. 65; © binkk7, p. 73; YOSHIKAZU TSUNO/AFP/Getty Images, p. 77; K. L. Howard/Alamy Stock Photo, p. 81; robertharding/Alamy Stock Photo, p. 83; SIMON HAYTER/TORONTO STAR/Getty Images, p. 87; Francesco Gustincich/Alamy Stock Photo, p. 96. Backgrounds: iStock.com/martin-dm; iStock.com/TommL, iStock.com/LanternWorks; iStock.com/FatCamera; iStock.com/jmbatt.

Front cover art: Shauna Lynn Panczyszyn.